TRANSACTIONS OF THE

AMERICAN PHILOSOPHICAL SOCIETY

HELD AT PHILADELPHIA

FOR PROMOTING USEFUL KNOWLEDGE

VOLUME 67, PART 7 · 1977

The Pioneer Stage
of Railroad Electrification

CARL W. CONDIT

PROFESSOR OF HISTORY, ART HISTORY, AND URBAN AFFAIRS,
NORTHWESTERN UNIVERSITY

THE AMERICAN PHILOSOPHICAL SOCIETY

INDEPENDENCE SQUARE: PHILADELPHIA

November, 1977

Copyright © 1977 by The American Philosophical Society

Library of Congress Catalog
Card Number 77-76428
International Standard Book Number 0–87169–677–0
US ISSN 0065–9746

THE PIONEER STAGE OF RAILROAD ELECTRIFICATION

CARL W. CONDIT

CONTENTS

PART I: 1895–1897

The creation of a reliable system of mass transportation operated by electric power, or more specifically by electric traction motors, was probably the most complex technological achievement of the nineteenth century, and by virtue of its internal complexity and its far-reaching consequences it was the supreme example of the technological revolution in the modern industrial period. The multitude of determinants that initially brought it about and then shaped its subsequent course ranged from the most advanced theoretical science at one end of the spectrum to virtually indefinable social and psychological responses at the other. Indeed, beside the introduction of a practical electric railway even the most thoroughgoing scientific revolution seems like a relatively simple and obvious event in intellectual history, although the full range of its future implications may far transcend the purely intellectual realm. As a medium of both intra-urban and interurban transportation on a scale commensurate with the needs of modern industrial societies, the electric railroad and rapid transit have proved to be the safest, most efficient, most appropriate to the contemporary environment, and most aesthetically satisfying of all the alternative forms; thus, for both its internal character and its implications, the history of electric traction deserves a thorough analytical investigation, but it has so far received from historians only the briefest and most superficial treatment.

The scope of the subject requires that the historian first establish the various phases of its development and then define the different forms of rail transportation to which the electric motor could be adapted. Electric traction is inseparable from the creation of the genera-

tor, central power generation, and the rotary motor, which is in essence a generator with its operation reversed. And these, as all historians of science and technology know, go back to the laboratory discoveries in electromagnetic induction made by Oersted, Faraday, Ampère, and Henry over the years from 1820 to 1831. There are four distinguishable modes of electric rail transit, of which the oldest of the practically successful forms is the street railway, its vehicle called a tram in England and a streetcar or trolley in the United States. The others in order of their chronological appearance are the intra-city rapid transit (if we regard the City and South London Railway as the first of its kind), the single-car interurban railway, and finally the electrified standard railroad, which was once universally operated by steam locomotives. My intention in this paper is to restrict myself to the electrification of the steam railroad in its pioneer phase, but in order to place it in its proper historical context it is necessary to examine its antecedents in the street and interurban railways. Experimental attempts to build electric locomotives for regular rail service antedate the first streetcars by a few years, but as we shall see in the course of this history, all such attempts proved abortive or at least unwanted on a continuing basis, so that the construction and operation of successful street and interurban cars proved to be the decisive events underlying the achievement of practical railroad electrification in 1895.

I. THE BACKGROUND HISTORY OF MOTORS AND ELECTRIC RAILWAYS

Another curiosity in the history of nineteenth-century technology is that attempts to build electrically powered vehicles antedated the invention of a reliable generator of electric power by nearly forty years. As a matter of fact, it was the reliance of the motor on the battery as a source of power that so restricted its range of operation as to render most such vehicles little more than laboratory curiosities when they were not outright financial and technical disasters.[1] The scientific basis

---

[1] Brief, reasonably reliable, but wholly inadequate secondary accounts of the early history of electric power generation, motors, and their railroad applications may be found in the appropriate sections of the following recent works: Percy Dunsheath, *A History of Electrical Engineering* (London, Faber and Faber, 1962); C. Mackechnie Jarvis, "The Generation of Electricity," in: Charles Singer *et al.*, eds., *A History of Technology,* 5 (Oxford, Clarendon Press, 1958): pp. 177–207; Malcolm MacLaren, *The Rise of the Electrical Industry in the Nineteenth Century* (Princeton, Princeton University Press,

of the electric motor was Oersted's demonstration in 1820 that a magnetized needle was made to rotate in the vicinity of a current-carrying wire, but the possibilities of technical application did not appear until Faraday constructed a laboratory apparatus around 1822 by which he caused a magnetized and pivoted wire to rotate in an electric field and a similar though electrically charged wire in a magnetic field. The continuous rotational movement was the important consequence, but in spite of this now obvious phenomenon, there were several earlier attempts to invent reciprocating motors, probably with the steam engine conceived as a model. If one could place one or more current-carrying loops in a magnetic field, arrange suitable connections between the movable loops and the stationary incoming conductor, and devise a reasonably reliable and steady source of power, one would have made a workable motor presumably capable of driving some kind of vehicle. It seemed to be a relatively simple matter compared to a steam locomotive, but it proved to be considerably more difficult than it appeared. The rotating loops were to become the armature; the magnetic poles, alternating north and south and arranged in a circular pattern, were to constitute the encompassing field, and the connection between the rotating loops and the power source (the incoming conductor), the commutator and its brushes.

Practical difficulties do not deter inventors, who either overlook them and generally fail or find ways to overcome them. Before the end of the decade in which Faraday made his celebrated discoveries Thomas Davenport of Brandon, Vermont, built an electrically operated railway (1835), Joseph Henry constructed a workable reciprocating motor (1837), and the Russian physicist and inventor H. M. Jacobi propelled a small boat by means of an electric motor (1838). The source of power in all cases was a battery, and it was to remain so until 1870 because the practical electric generator proved to be a more refractory problem than the motor. The first electric locomotive to be operated on standard railroad tracks was built by Robert Davidson of Aberdeen, Scotland, in 1838–1839, a five-ton machine powered by forty batteries which must have constituted a major part of the weight. The embryo of the third-rail system for supplying the locomotive with power came with various French patents granted in 1845 to Alexandre Bessolo, but details have not to

FIG. 1. Moses G. Farmer's electric locomotive of 1847. A photograph of a partly conjectural model in the Smithsonian Institution. (Smithsonian Institution)

my knowledge appeared in any secondary accounts.[2]

An invention that perhaps proved more valuable for the ultimate development of useful electric traction was the locomotive built by Moses G. Farmer at Dover, New Hampshire, and used strictly for experimental purposes in connection with the inventor's lectures on electricity (fig. 1). This primitive object was little more than a crude platform on two four-wheel trucks, but it embodied at least one feature that was later to prove essential in a traction system. The power again was provided by a battery that was enclosed in a wooden box at the rear of the platform. The armature coils lay isolated at the ends of the spokes of a wheel-like form, and the field coils, of which there

1943); William D. Middleton, *When the Steam Railroads Electrified* (Milwaukee, Kalmbach Publishing Company, 1974); Harold Passer, *The Electrical Manufacturers, 1875–1900* (Cambridge, Harvard University Press, 1953); Harold Sharlin, "Applications of Electricity" and "Electrical Generation and Transmission," in: Melvin Kranzberg and Carroll Pursell, eds., *Technology in Western Civilization* (New York, Oxford University Press, 1967) 1: chs. 34, 35; Harold Sharlin, *The Making of the Electrical Age* (New York, Abelard-Schumann, 1964).

[2] With one exception, none of the inventions belonging to what we might call the primitive phase of electric locomotion has properly engaged the attention of historians. In addition to the works cited in note 1 brief and superficial accounts of these inventions may be found in the following: E. H. Bentley, "Brief History of Electric and Magnetic Locomotion," *Scientific American*, **5**, 10 (6 September, 1884): p. 153; "Electric Traction," *Encyclopaedia Britannica* (11th ed., New York, Encyclopaedia Britannica Publishing Company, 1910); C. Hamilton Ellis, "Underground and Electric Railways," in: Charles Singer, *op. cit.* **5**: pp. 346–348.

appear to have been four, were located under the lower third of the armature in a thoroughly inefficient manner. The control was simply a switch that opened or closed the battery circuit. What was important was the use of gearing to transmit the torque of the armature to the wheels, a technique that was the forerunner of all the geared drives of cars and locomotives. But the vulnerable and soon exhausted battery prevented Farmer's locomotive from reaching any commercial success.[3]

The same limitation proved the undoing of the much more spectacular machine built by Charles G. Page in 1851 and given a test run on a standard railroad line.[4] Weighing 10.5 tons, with a wheel arrangement divided into a pilot truck and driving wheels, like that of a steam locomotive, and powered by a 100-cell battery, Page's invention suggested something of the successful forms that were to come at the end of the century. The 21-foot length of the engine was covered by a windowed box cab providing room for a few passengers as well as the operating elements. The driving mechanism was unfortunately another based on an analogy to the steam engine: a solenoid wound as a hollow cylinder surrounded a cylindrical bar of iron large enough to have weighed about 250 pounds. On the opening of the control switch the current flowed into the solenoid and drew the bar into the hollow core; when the switch was closed the bar returned to its original position. Cross-head guides like those of a steam engine kept the piston in line, and a connecting rod and crank converted its reciprocal motion into the rotary motion of the driving axle. The locomotive was given its initial and final test run over the tracks of the Baltimore and Ohio Railroad at Bladensburg, Maryland, on 29 April, 1851. The experiment ended in disaster: improper counterbalancing, the absence of spring suspension, and rough track produced shocks that broke the ceramic diaphragms of the battery, while overheating damaged the insulation of the solenoid coils which resulted in the short-circuiting of the mechanism. Page was backed by the federal government, but the project was a failure, and forty-four years were to pass before the B. and O. inaugurated the world's first successful railroad electrification.

These early inventions were isolated events, forming no progressive pattern, with the consequence that they all proved abortive because the unreliable battery power offered no commercial possibilities. Success in the development of electric traction for railroad purposes could thus come only with two prior inventions, namely, the rotary motor with its armature and field coils wound in such a way as to secure the most efficient utilization of the immense mechanical power latent in the electric field, and the generator operating continuously at a sustained high voltage. Inventors had been busy with the generator since 1832, but the solution to all essential problems, or at least partial solutions pointing in the right direction, came with the development of a practical heavy-duty generator by Zénobe Théophile Gramme in 1870.[5] The background to this achievement was an international enterprise, with British, French, Italian, Belgian, German, and American engineers and scientists playing decisive roles. What is more to our theme, however, is that Gramme also built the first practical motor by realizing that if he had a workable generator he also in effect possessed the motor by reversing the mode of operation. In 1873 Gramme and Hippolyte Fontaine exhibited at a Viennese exposition a pair of direct-current generators in which the current produced by one caused the armature coils of the other to rotate in its own magnetic field. The consequence was another irony in this peculiarly complex process: a workable direct-current motor was available before the engineers had solved the problem of the large-scale generation and distribution of electric power. The alternating-current generator (A. de Meritens in France, 1881) and motor (Nikola Tesla in the United States, 1888), with their essential concomitant, the alternating-current transformer (Lucien Gaulard and John D. Gibbs in England, 1882), greatly extended the useful possibilities of electrical machinery.

Although the creation of the electric motor was the work of inventors aiming at utilitarian results, the theoretical concepts underlying it stood at the very frontier of physical science. It was no coincidence that the invention of Gramme and Fontaine appeared in the same year as that of Maxwell's *Treatise on Electricity and Magnetism* (1873). Though Maxwell had rejected his earlier model of the electromagnetic field (1861–1862) in favor of a purely mathematical description thereof in the form of his celebrated equations, the model, for all its contradictions, offered the only conceivable explanation in physical terms of the behavior of generators and motors. Maxwell posited the existence of longitudinal tubes or vortices of magnetism normally in a state of rotation. Lying between them were contiguous spheres of electricity which served, like idler gears, to maintain the magnetic rotations in the same direction. A change in the strength of the field, conceived as an increase or decrease in rotational velocity, caused an increase in the similar velocity of the spheres accompanied by a longitudinal tension in turn causing a movement along the axial line,

---

[3] The best source of information that I know of on Farmer's locomotive is the model and accompanying legend in the Smithsonian Institution's Museum of History and Technology.

[4] Page's invention has been the only one to receive proper attention from a historian. A full account of the genesis and the test run may be found in Robert C. Post, "The Page Locomotive: Federal Sponsorship of Invention in Mid-Nineteenth Century America," *Technology and Culture* 13, 2 (April, 1972). pp. 140–169.

---

[5] See C. Mackechnie Jarvis, "The Generation of Electricity," in: Singer, *op. cit.,* pp. 177–207. Later historians seem agreed that no new evidence has so far turned up to invalidate the claim of Gramme's preeminence.

or a current of electricity. Conversely, a change in the current strength would cause a corresponding change in the strength—that is, torque or rotational power—of the magnetic field. A generator, then, is a device that introduces a constant rhythmic change into the magnetic field, causing a similar rhythmic flow of electrical particles in the containing vessel or circuit. The explanation of the action of the motor requires considerably greater imagination and has not been attempted in detail in terms of Maxwell's field model. One must assume that the mechanical connection between electricity and magnetism in the model is of such a kind that rotary motion of the conductor will occur when the current-carrying element is placed contiguous to the rotating cylindrical vortices of the field.

With Gramme's reliable motor available in 1873, and with its form and operation widely publicized through international expositions and the new scientific and engineering journals, it seemed likely that a continuously operable electric locomotive would appear in a few years. The forerunner of all subsequent developments was the little electric railway constructed by Ernst Werner von Siemens for the International Trades Exposition that opened in Berlin on 31 May, 1879.[6] The line consisted of a circular track 300 meters in length, and the power was distributed by means of a third rail in the form of a flat iron bar laid on the center line of the track. The return circuit was the running rails themselves, specially bonded at the joints for the unimpeded flow of the current. The little four-wheel locomotive was equipped with a direct-current motor operating at 150 volts, which developed three horsepower at 4.2 miles per hour. The drum armature was set with its axis in the longitudinal direction, and the rotation was transmitted to the driving axle by means of two sets of conical gears. The railway safely carried 86,398 passengers in the four months that the exposition remained open, but the evidence suggests that the public showed little enthusiasm for transforming this novelty into a permanent installation and was actually afraid of possible harm to anyone standing in the vicinity of electrical conductors. This lack of interest failed to deter the inventor, however, and his firm of Siemens and Halske opened a street railway line at Gross Lichterfelde, near Berlin, on 16 May,

1881, to provide the world with the first public commercial carrier operated by electric power.[7]

The Berlin achievements ushered in an extremely prolific decade which saw the establishment of extensive street railway systems operated by electric power, appearing almost simultaneously with repeated though ultimately abortive attempts to develop reliable electric locomotion for standard railroads. An industrial switching locomotive drawing power from a storage battery was placed in operation at a linen-bleaching plant at Breuil-en-Auge, France, in 1881, to be followed the next year by the manufacture of the first battery-powered streetcar, for service in Vincennes, France. Two small electric railways designed for seaside vacationers appeared in the British Isles in 1883, the earlier at Brighton, the later and longer line at the Giant's Causeway, near Portrush, Ireland. The latter was the first for which power was generated by water turbines, located in this case at a falls in the River Rush. The most important accomplishment, however, was again the work of Siemens and Halske. The company in 1884 built a street railway line between Frankfurt-am-Main and Offenbach, Germany, characterized by two innovations of lasting value: one was the overhead trolley with a return in a slotted pipelike conduit between the rails, and the other was the two-car unit divided between motor car and trailer.[8]

Meanwhile, three American inventors were equally active in the promising though still unfamiliar territory. Stephen D. Field laid down an electric railway at Stockbridge, Massachusetts, early in 1880 in which power was distributed through a third rail placed in an underground conduit covered by a slotted plate through which the contactor was inserted. This device later became common among street railway systems located in cities where overhead wires were considered undesirable, as in Washington, D. C., for the most notable example. In the year of Field's Stockbridge venture Thomas Edison built a 1,400-foot electric line at Menlo Park, New Jersey, with the power supply distributed through one running rail and the return through the other, the two necessarily being insulated from each other. Field and Edison pooled their talents

---

[6] Siemens's achievements were quickly publicized in the press of Europe and America. See, for example, "Electrical Railway," *Scientific American* **42**, 9 (28 February, 1880): p. 137. Siemens received so much attention, as a matter of fact, that the editors of *Scientific American* were moved by a patriotic spirit to recall earlier inventions and to assert that the United States was really ahead of Europe in such matters and could look forward to a promising future. See "The Electric Railway an American Invention," *Scientific American* **42**, 22 (29 May, 1880): pp. 336–337, and "The Future of the Electric Railway," *loc. cit.* **42**, 24 (12 June, 1880): p. 368. See also "The Early Electric Railway Work of Werner von Siemens," *Street Railway Jour.* **24**, 15 (8 October, 1904): pp. 535–536.

[7] "Opening of the Electric Railway in Berlin," *Scientific American* **44**, 22 (28 May, 1881): p. 336. The distribution system also involved the third rail located on the center line of the tracks.

[8] Articles on the work of this early period offering more details than the existing histories of technology are the following: S. T. Dodd, "Development of Railway Motor Design," *Street Railway Jour.* **24**, 15 (8 October, 1904): pp. 551–555, and "Evolution of the Electric Railway Motor," *loc. cit.* **22**, 26 (26 December, 1903): pp. 1092–1096; Eugene Griffin, "The Beginnings of the Electric Railway Motor," *loc. cit.* **24**, 15 (8 October, 1904): pp. 575–579; William D. Middleton, "Electricity Challenges Steam," *op. cit.*, pp. 10–35. The Brighton Beach line is described in "The Electric Railway at Brighton," *Scientific American* **49**, 15 (13 October, 1883): p. 233, and **50**, 24 (14 June, 1884): p. 371.

and their resources in 1882, when they founded the Electric Railway Company of the United States, but in spite of the fact that the now famous inventor enjoyed the backing of Henry Villard, president of the Northern Pacific Railway, the new venture failed, or rather, died for lack of further activity. The bankruptcy of the Northern Pacific was a minor contributing factor; the chief reason for the collapse was that both Edison and Villard believed that the future of electrification lay in light-traffic branch lines scattered as mainline feeders through the agricultural West. While this program might have proved a boon to the farmers if anyone could have afforded the cost, it stood in absolute contrast to the cardinal principle of all the officers of electrified railroads in the days when the new technique finally established itself—namely, that electrification is feasible only in areas of the highest population, traffic, and commercial density, the three ordinarily occurring together.[9]

The third of the three inventors enjoyed considerably greater success and contributed valuable innovations to the infancy of street railway development. Leo Daft, who founded the Daft Electric Company at Greenville, New Jersey, in 1881, began experimental work with electric locomotives in the same year and achieved something of a triumph in 1883, when a machine manufactured for the Saratoga and Mount McGregor Railroad in New York easily hauled a fully loaded coach up a 1.5 per cent grade.[10] This modest but convincing accomplishment paved the way to Daft's greatest opportunity. In 1885 his company received the contract for the electrification of the Baltimore–Hampden, Maryland, branch of the Union Passenger Railroad Company, which thus became the first commercial electric railroad in the United States, if we distinguish it from street railways by virtue of the presence of separate motive power hauling unpowered cars. The Hampden line offered formidable challenges, with its almost unbroken curves and grades up to 6.63 per cent, but Daft met them satisfactorily: his first two locomotives were delivered on 15 August, 1885, and these were followed by two more a year later. The whole installation embodied increasingly familiar features—direct-current motors wired for a potential of 260 volts, geared drive, and center-line third-rail distribution of power. In the spring of 1886 Daft received two patents for

innovations on the Baltimore–Hampden line of decisive importance for the subsequent evolution of the art: one was the overhead conductor or trolley wire, previously introduced on the Continent by Siemens at Frankfurt, and the other was its necessary concomitant, the under-running trolley. The Hampden line reverted to horsecar operation in 1889, but among the passengers in that first summer of 1885 was John K. Cowen, chief counsel of the Baltimore and Ohio Railroad, which was to bring about the revolution ten years later with the electrification of its Baltimore Belt line.

Another locomotive from Daft's plant at Greenville, originally built in 1885, was tested on the Ninth Avenue elevated line in New York during the latter part of that year and in the summer of 1886. Rebuilt in 1888, the new machine was given an enlarged and rewired motor to increase the voltage from 300 to 450 and the capacity from 75 to 128 horsepower, and an additional pair of driving wheels connected to the first pair by side rods, a forerunner of the drive system employed in the first electric locomotives of the Pennsylvania Railroad's New York extension. Still another novelty from the Greenville works was a locomotive manufactured in 1887 and equipped with side-rod drive and gears for use on a Pittsburgh rack railroad with 15 per cent grades. It was placed in service in August, 1888, by which date the decisive events in railroad electrification were occurring in the new street railway and underground installations.

The first street railway to be constructed in the United States as a public carrier deliberately designed to compete with the ruling horsecar was the line laid down in Cleveland, Ohio, by E. H. Bentley and Walter Knight and opened for service in the summer of 1884.[11] Another entrant into the field, Charles J. Van Depoele, proved more ambitious in his introduction of experimental trolley lines in Toronto, Canada, and Detroit, South Bend, and Minneapolis in the United States, during the years 1884–1885. They attracted enough favorable attention to win him the contract for what was then called a city-wide system in Montgomery, Alabama. His chief innovation, one which found continuous use throughout street railway history, was the rigid, spring-activated trolley pole that held a grooved wheel tightly against the overhead wire.[12] Other smaller excursions, all tentative and experimental whether their authors intended this character or not, followed during the next few years. A short-lived and rather primitive line was installed in Kansas City by John C. Henry (1885–1887), and a battery-powered car manufactured by the Belgian engineer Edmond Julien in 1886 was tested in New York, Boston, and

---

[9] Edison's work receives some attention, with appropriate illustrations, in Middleton, *op. cit.*, and his failure is well analyzed in Passer, *op. cit.*, pp. 219–223. See also "Electric Railway Work in America Prior to 1888," *Street Railway Jour.* 24, 15 (8 October, 1904): pp. 559–562.

[10] The sources for Daft's achievements are the following: Leo Daft, "The Early Work of the Daft Company," *Street Railway Jour.* 24, 15 (8 October, 1904): pp. 528–534; "Electric Motor on the New York Elevated Railroad," *Scientific American* 53, 21 (21 November, 1885): pp. 319, 326; "Electric Railway," *loc. cit.* 49, 23 (8 December, 1883), p. 352; "Electric Railway Work in America Prior to 1888," *Street Railway Jour.* 24, 15 (8 October, 1904), pp. 559–562.

[11] "Opening of a New Electric Street Railroad," *Scientific American* 51, 6 (9 August, 1884): p. 84.

[12] Van Depoele's work is considered in the standard histories; see also "The Van Depoele Electric Railway," *Scientific American* 54, 1 (2 January, 1886): p. 7.

Saint Louis in the next two years.[13] The ironic result was that the tests had the effect of administering the *coup de grace* to battery power. It offered the advantage of sparing the company the enormous investment in generating, substation, transmission, and distribution equipment, but the delicate batteries were easily broken, and Julien's inefficient and jolting chain drive increased the impact of shocks arising from switches and rough rail.

The precarious installations of the early eighties proved to be preliminary essays to the climactic event in American railroad electrification of every category. The inventor, physical scientist, electrical engineer and enterpreneur Frank Julian Sprague, who had joined Edison's staff at Menlo Park in 1883 and founded the Sprague Electric Railway and Motor Company in 1884, was awarded the seemingly impossible contract in 1887 to build the twelve-mile Richmond, Virginia, street railway in ninety days. His previous experience in the field had been confined to experiments in electric traction conducted in 1885–1886 on test tracks of the Manhattan Elevated Railway Company.[14] But for all the limitations of his experience, Sprague appeared to have a more thorough grasp of the realities, difficulties, and potentialities of the electric motor than many of his contemporaries. The problems that had to be solved for operation in the hilly topography of Richmond were chiefly the mounting and enclosure of the motor to withstand shocks and protect the working parts from dirt and moisture, the form and mounting of commutator ring and brushes for the same ends, the design of trolley pole to maintain tight and continuous contact with the wire, and a control system that would suppress the destructive arcs that accompanied the heavy surges of current necessary to start cars on steep grades. Sprague's primary solution was a compact, enclosed yet accessible motor suspended on one side by a sleeve bearing on the axle and on the other by a stout coil spring fixed to the truck frame (fig. 2). The drive was a simple but rugged gear-and-pinion form that transmitted the aramature torque to the axle with a minimum of slippage and jolting. If not all the problems were perfectly solved, the way had been so clearly marked out that others needed only to follow the obvious signposts. The Richmond line opened in 1888 on schedule but at a cost of $70,000 to Sprague. Success came to him the following year when Henry C. Whitney of Boston ordered Sprague equipment for all the street railway mileage that Whitney had laid down in the city.

In the very year of Sprague's achievement at Richmond, however, a potent competitor quickly emerged to win a preeminent position. The electrical manufacturing company founded by Elihu Thomson and Edwin J. Houston at Lynn, Massachusetts, in 1883 began the manufacture of railway equipment in 1888. The production of cars for the modest street railway system of Lynn in the same year was followed in 1889 by the enviable contract to equip the new street car lines of Washington, D. C. By 1890 the Sprague and Thomson-Houston companies dominated the field: of the 8,000 streetcars manufactured through 1892 Sprague provided electrical equipment for 28.75 per cent and the Thomson firm for 34.6 per cent, for a combined total of nearly two-thirds of the industry product. As convincing as the practical demonstration was the result of a comparative study of costs made by Eugene Griffin, head of Thomson-Houston's railway department, and published in 1888. It spelled the end of the horsecar and the cable railway, for the cost of operating and maintaining a horse and car on a per-mile basis ·turned out to range as high as three times the cost of operating the existing forms of electric street railways.[15] The Thomson-Houston and the Edison General Electric companies were merged in 1892 to form the General Electric Corporation, and in 1893 the new firm began the manufacture of electric locomotives for standard railroad service.

The practical success and the low cost of streetcar operation quickly led to the interurban railway as the next logical development. In 1891 the Minneapolis Street Railway Company and the Saint Paul City Railway established a joint operation connecting the two cities which was literally interurban but largely confined to urban streets. Something more nearly like the

[13] "Electric Street Cars in New York City," *Scientific American* **59**, 14 (6 October, 1888) : p. 209.

[14] Sprague's career is treated in a monograph by Harold C. Passer, "Frank Julian Sprague," in: William Miller, ed., *Men in Business* (Cambridge, Harvard University Press, 1952), and in Sprague's brief autobiographical reminiscences, "Some Personal Experiences," *Street Railway Jour.* **24**, 15 (8 October, 1904): pp. 566–575. Fuller secondary treatments of the Richmond street railway are in Percy Dunsheath, *op. cit.,* pp. 184–185, and Harold Sharlin, "Applications of Electricity," in: Kranzberg and Pursell, *op. cit.,* pp. 572–573. A well-illustrated source is *The Electric Street Railway System at Richmond, Va.* (Richmond, Richmond Union Passenger Railway Company, 1889).

[15] The comparative costs in Griffin's analysis are given in the following table:

| | Electrical operation | | | | |
	Overhead conductor	Conduit conductor	Battery	Cable car	Horse car
Investment per mile of track (construction and equipment)	$23,400	$40,400	$38,500	$56,650	$20,200
Annual Operating Expense per mile of track	3,325	5,025	8,862	8,508	10,682

(Source: Passer, *Electrical Manufacturers,* p. 254.) See also "Rapid Progress of Electric Railways," *Scientific American* **65**, 22 (28 November, 1891): p. 344.

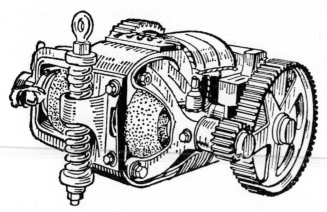

FIG. 2. The motor designed by Frank J. Sprague for the Richmond Union Passenger Railway, 1887–1888. (Dunsheath, *A History of Electrical Engineering*)

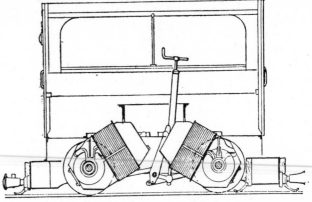

FIG. 3. Longitudinal section of the locomotive built for the City and South London Railway, 1887–1890. (Dunsheath, *A History of Electrical Engineering*)

open-country operation of the conventional interurban came with the opening of the East Side Railway's Portland-Oregon City line and the Sandusky, Milan and Norwalk Railway's line uniting those cities in Ohio, both in 1893. The first interurban road to use separate motor cars as distinct from unmotorized trailers was the Kentucky and Indiana Bridge Company, which initiated operations in the same year.[16] They marked the modest beginnings of what proved to be the most rapidly expanding form of mass transportation. Sprague's invention of multiple-unit control over the years 1892 to 1897, by means of which any number of motor cars could be controlled by a single motorman, was the decisive factor in leading to a similar expansion of electrified rapid transit service in the larger cities.[17]

The European development that corresponded in its historical role to Sprague's achievement at Richmond was the City and South London Railway, constructed under the direction of James H. Greathead and Peter W. Barlow in 1887–1890 as the world's first underground railway designed as a public carrier. Moreover, although it was exclusively a rapid-transit operation, it was the first regularly operated public railroad line in which the cars were pulled by separate locomotives. These little four-wheel machines were equipped with two 25-horsepower motors wired to draw direct current at a pressure of 500 volts (fig. 3). The individual engine could haul a 40-ton three-car train at the creditable speed of 25 miles per hour, a rate probably exceeding the normal speed of the steam-powered elevated

trains of New York City. The motors of the London locomotives involved several innovative features of value for the subsequent evolution of the art. The armatures were the ring variety developed by Gramme, and they rotated in a bipolar magnetic field that was rather clumsily and inefficiently arranged. Field and armature were series wound, as opposed to the earlier shunt-wound forms. Most important for the eventual progress in driving mechanisms was the elimination of gearing by mounting the armature directly on the locomotive axle.[18]

What we might call the adolescent phase of the pioneer stage was rounded out by two attempts to exploit electric traction to satisfy the American lust for speed. The first proved astonishingly prophetic, but the second never advanced beyond the stage of a preliminary announcement. In 1889 David G. Weems and Oscar T. Crosby (Sprague's principal associate in the Richmond enterprise) built a small four-wheel two-motor locomotive for experimental operation on a track of 28-inch gage laid down for the purpose at Laurel, Maryland. Drawing power at 500 volts from an overhead third rail and set in motion or stopped by means of a switch in the generating station (the first remote control), the two inventors were able to raise the speed of the machine to 115 miles per hour. Crosby's ideas

---

[16] The standard work on the history of interurban railways is George W. Hilton and John F. Due, *The Electric Interurban Railway in America* (Stanford, Stanford University Press, 1960). For numerous illustrations of interurban cars, see William D. Middleton, *The Interurban Era* (Milwaukee, Kalmbach Publishing Company, 1961). See also "Minneapolis Electric Street Railway," *Scientific American* **65**, 10 (5 September, 1891) : p. 147.

[17] Frank J. Sprague, "The Multiple Unit System for Electric Railways," *Cassier's Magazine* **16**, 4 (August, 1899) : pp. 460–468.

[18] The City and South London motive power is briefly described in Dunsheath, *op. cit.*, and by C. Hamilton Ellis, in Singer, *op. cit.* In a series-wound motor the field and the armature are connected in series, so that current under the given potential passes from the field to the armature; in the shunt-wound form the two are in parallel, and the voltage is divided between them. The series form is superior in providing a maximum tractive effort through the rotative force or torque of the armature. The parallel wiring of the shunt-wound motor produces excessive hysteresis, that is, the lag in magnetization behind the magnetizing agency, which is the current that creates the electromagnetic field of the motor poles. The result is a kind of electrical friction that prevents the realization of the full torque for the current drawn. The question of the geared versus the gearless drive was to become a major controversy by the turn of the century (see below).

for high-speed rail service were prophetic but empirically and technologically premature: he proposed regenerative braking, magnetic brakes, all-steel cars, and streamlining by means of paraboloidal front ends and unbroken car sides—all eventually developed but in some cases far into the new century. Wellington Adams sought to translate this demonstrated capacity for high speeds into practical reality in his plan of 1892 to build a double-track line on an unbroken tangent between Chicago and Saint Louis on which electrically powered cars were to be operated at 100 miles per hour. Adams's proposal was not taken seriously by the editors of the technical press, but in truth he offered a number of valuable concepts that again were to be realized only in the distant future. His intention to eliminate all grade crossings and to operate trains on an exclusive right of way involved the complete separation of different transportation modes and of high-speed through traffic from local runs. His plan to build highways on either side of the railroad line represented the first transportation corridor, described in more sophisticated form in Burnham and Bennett's *Plan of Chicago* (1909) and not finally realized until the completion of Congress Expressway in that city (1958).[19]

II. THE BALTIMORE AND OHIO ELECTRIFICATION

It was historically appropriate that the first electrification of a steam railroad main line should have been placed in service by the Baltimore and Ohio Railroad, since it was the first railroad company to operate trains in the United States, and equally appropriate that the achievement should have been made in Baltimore, where Leo Daft had already introduced the electrical operation of passenger vehicles. The technological preparation for this revolution I have sketched in the first part of this article, but the precise events that impelled the railroad company toward taking so drastic a step began to occur twelve years before the new installation was made and composed a dense complex of social, urbanistic, economic, and technical factors. For more than fifty years after it inaugurated regular train service (1830) the eastern terminal of the B. and O. was located at Baltimore, where the Camden Station (1852–1856) served as the passenger terminal. Early in 1883 the company launched an ambitious program that aimed at extending its lines to the lucrative traffic potential of the Philadelphia area and, it was hoped, New York Harbor. On 31 January the directors organized the Baltimore and Philadelphia Railroad to construct a line to Philadelphia, and before the end of the year they

acquired and merged the partly constructed Delaware Western Railroad. The completion of the whole program came three years later, so that the Philadelphia line was opened to service on 19 September, 1886. Meanwhile, the railroad set in motion the corporate and legal machinery by which it hoped to extend the new line into the New York Harbor area, the end of the rainbow sought by every railroad within a day's travel of the city. In a succession of moves through 1885–1886 the B. and O. acquired trackage rights from Park Junction, Philadelphia, to Bound Brook, New Jersey, over the Philadelphia and Reading Railroad, and from Bound Brook to Jersey City over the Central Railroad of New Jersey, and organized the Baltimore and New York Railroad to construct the extension that would take it on a straight easterly course from Cranford, New Jersey, to the west edge of Staten Island, later to be Richmond Borough of New York City. The building of the new line was accomplished in 1887–1889, and in the latter year the B. and O. acquired a controlling interest in the Staten Island Rapid Transit and its subsidiary, the Staten Island Railway, to bring its cars to the water's edge in New York Harbor.[20]

The opening of the line to Philadelphia brought a rapid increase in traffic, but the B. and O.'s line through Baltimore proved to be more of a bottleneck than an artery for the expeditious movement of freight and passengers. The central area of the city, immediately north of its original core, lies on a low domelike hill that could not be surmounted and had either to be bypassed or tunneled. The B. and O. main track, as a consequence, lay along the waterfront, with the broad estuary of the Patapsco River North West Branch lying directly across its eastern continuation (fig. 4). The crossing could only be negotiated by train ferry and car float, an expensive, time-consuming operation that placed the company at a serious competitive disadvantage. Moreover, the line east of the Patapsco River crossing was located in a densely built commercial, industrial, and inner-city residential area where the main tracks were threaded through an unbroken succession of yards, spurs, and sidings. The first plan of the railroad's engineering department was the elevation of the line east of the river, but it was abandoned because of a combination of financial and urbanistic factors: the high cost of land discouraged the company directors, and the destruction of the urban fabric along with the obstruc-

[19] "The Weems Electric Railway," *Engineering News* 22, 11 (14 September, 1889): pp. 250–251; "One Hundred Miles an Hour by Electricity," *Scientific American* 66, 11 (12 March, 1892): p. 161. Sprague had proposed a high-density main-line electric service of two-car high-speed trains as early as 1890, but it was another five years before the first and highly tentative steps were taken ["Electro-Motors on Trunk Lines," *Scientific American* 62, 9 (1 March, 1890): p. 130].

[20] The construction of the B. and O.'s New York extension was a costly undertaking because it included in its 6.5-mile length 13,146 feet 6 inches of timber trestles, iron girder bridges, and iron truss bridges, including the 496-foot 6-inch swing span over Arthur Kill. Thus 38 per cent of the line was made up of bridges and trestle-work, all of it founded on extensive piling because of the alluvial and marine sediments of the north Jersey shore areas. The numerous bridges were designed by Charles Ackenheil, chief engineer of the Baltimore and New York Railroad. ["The Arthur Kill Bridge," *Railroad Gazette* 20 (22 June, 1888): pp. 399–400; "The Arthur Kill Bridge Approaches," *loc. cit.* 21 (26 July, 1889): pp. 488–489].

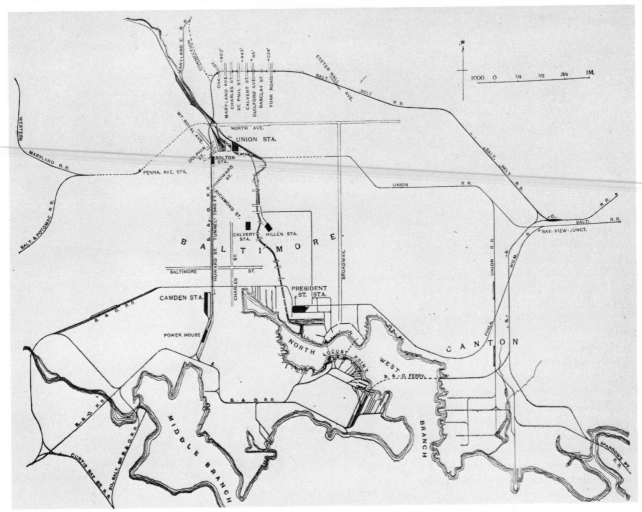

Fig. 4. Map showing the Baltimore and Ohio Railroad lines in Baltimore
at the time of the electrification of 1895. (*Railroad Gazette*)

tion to traffic flow on streets and rail lines and the difficult problem of reaching industrial spurs would have proved intolerable to the city as well as the railroad. Another factor that helped to induce the directors to make a thoroughgoing revision of the Baltimore trackage arose from demographic changes within the city. The population and the intensive commercial development of the inner city were shifting northward, away from the waterfront, which suggested to the railroad officers the advantage, if not the eventual necessity, of building a new station 1½ miles north of the Camden facility.

On 17 December, 1888, with the New York extension well in progress, the directors decided to build an entirely new line connecting Camden Station with the projected Mount Royal Station to the north on a direct tangent between the two, then turning eastward to Bay View Junction and a connection with the recently opened line to Philadelphia. The B. and O. organized a construction subsidiary with the title of Baltimore Belt Railroad, initiated work in 1889, and brought the line

and the new station to completion in 1895 at a cost of $6,000,000.[21] The new route was a mile longer than the old, but it saved at least twenty minutes in running time and offered substantial reductions in the cost of operating trains through the city. The contruction program included the elimination of all grade crossings in Baltimore by means of an almost unbroken succession of cuts, bridges, and tunnels. These great advantages to both city and railroad, however, were secured only at the price of a serious operating prob-

[21] "Baltimore Belt Line Station and Equipment," *Railroad Gazette* 27 (28 June, 1895): p. 424; "The Baltimore Belt Line Tunnel," *loc. cit.* 27 (10 May, 1895): p. 302; "The Baltimore Belt Railroad," *loc. cit.* 26 (14 December, 1894): pp. 846–848; "The New Baltimore and Ohio Station in Baltimore," *loc. cit.* 28 (15 May, 1896): pp. 338–339; "Portals of the Howard Street Tunnel, Baltimore," *loc. cit.* 27 (11 January, 1895): pp. 18–19; "Recent Improvements on the Baltimore and Ohio: Terminal Improvements at Baltimore," *loc. cit.* 29, 42 (15 October, 1897): pp. 718–719. The replacement cost at the 1977 price level would be about $146,000,000.

FIG. 5. A Baltimore and Ohio train drawn by an electric locomotive, 1895. The photograph also shows the trolley and the overhead distribution system. (Smithsonian Institution, Chaney Collection)

lem. The penetration of Baltimore's central hill required a tunnel (officially identified as Howard Street Tunnel) 7,339 feet long, its floor lying on an average ascending grade of 0.8 per cent in the eastward direction. Other shorter tunnels raised the total length of underground track to 9,911 feet, and topographic irregularities required a short ruling grade of 1.52 per cent along the way. A 1½-mile shallow tunnel, marked by openings along its length, could probably have been ventilated well enough to save passengers and crew from asphyxiation, but the process would have proved intolerable to contiguous property owners.[22] The only solution was the operation at least of eastbound trains by the smoke-free electric traction, which had already proved itself in a similar situation though at a much reduced scale in the City and South London Railway. The Baltimore program was to be the real thing, a test case of a revolutionary form of standard railroad motive power with world-wide implications.

The B. and O. entered into a contract with the General Electric Company late in 1892 for a complete electrical installation over the length of the tunnel section of the Baltimore Belt Railroad, including locomotives, and generating, converting, transmission, and distribution

equipment. The designer of the locomotives was Louis Duncan of General Electric, and the engineer in charge of constructing the electrical facilities was Lee H. Parker of the railroad company. The first trial run was made on 27 June, 1894; the line was completed under power on 1 May, 1895, and regular service with three locomotives began on 1 August, 1895, the whole installation having cost the railroad about $8,000,000 (at least $194,000,000 at the 1977 price level).[23] The specifications set forth in the contract with General Electric called for an overhead trolley on the locomotive to pick up current from the distribution system, two four-wheel trucks with a direct-current motor on each axle rated at 300 horsepower, gearless drive, spring mounting on the truck frame, and iron-clad field poles with windings in mica-lined slots. The locomotives were designed, again according to specifications, to operate in either direction as two-part articulated units hauling 15 loaded passenger cars at 35 miles per hour or 30 loaded freight cars at 15 miles per hour up the 0.8 per cent grade, and they were equipped with air brakes and double cab control units that operated by progressively reducing the resistance built into the motor circuit. The total weight of 95 tons made the individual unit the heaviest locomotive manufactured up to that time, but more than half this weight, or 101,640 pounds, was accounted for by the motors alone. Most impressive was the high tractive effort of 47,500 pounds for what seemed a comparatively small machine (fig. 5). The general form of the exterior covering was that of the so-called steeple-cab locomotive in which a centrally located cab housing controls and indicators stood above the downward sloping ends. The form was restricted to switching and interurban service after 1900

---

[22] The Howard Street Tunnel was designed for four tracks, with the generous interior dimensions of 27 feet in width by 22 feet minimum overhead clearance. It was thought to be the longest tunnel at the time to be mined in soft soil, which in Baltimore is a mixture principally of sand, clay, gravel, loam, and disintegrated rock. On the question of ventilation, the necessary shafts would have presented no great problem, but the municipal ordinances authorizing the construction specifically prohibited the railroad from adopting the practice. A similar situation in the poorly ventilated Park Avenue Tunnel in New York, already an object of vehement criticism by the public, was eventually to lead to the largest of all terminal electrifications.

The directions in my description are used in the railroad sense: eastward is toward New York, westward toward Wheeling, regardless of the compass direction of train movement.

[23] The Baltimore electrification understandably drew considerable attention from the engineering press. The important sources are the following: "The Baltimore and Ohio Third-Rail System," *Railway Age* 34, 4 (25 July, 1902): pp. 93–96; "The Baltimore Tunnel Electric Locomotive in Service," *Railroad Gazette* 27 (4 October, 1895): p. 657; "The B. & O. Electric Locomotive," *loc. cit.* 27 (8 November, 1895): pp. 735–736; J. H. Davis, "The Baltimore and Ohio Electrification," *General Electric Rev.* 17, 11 (November, 1914): pp. 1083–1089; Louis Duncan, "The Substitution of Electricity for Steam in Railroad Practice," *Railroad Gazette* 27 (5 July, 1895): pp. 444–447; "Electrical Equipment of the Baltimore Belt Line Tunnel," *loc. cit.* 27 (19 July, 1895): pp. 480–482; "Electrical Equipment of the B. and O. Tunnel," *loc. cit.* 33, 2 (11 January, 1901): p. 30; "Hauling Trains by Electricity," *loc. cit.* 27 (21 June, 1895): p. 412; "Large Electric and Steam Locomotive," *Street Railway Jour.* 27, 8 (24 February, 1906): pp. 307–310; "Operation of the Baltimore and Ohio Electrification," *Electric Railway Jour.* 47, 24 (10 June, 1916): pp. 1074–1079; "The Working of an Electric Railroad," *Railroad Gazette* 27 (2 August, 1895): p. 516; W. D. Young, "The Third Rail on the Baltimore and Ohio," *Street Railway Jour.* 21, 11 (14 March, 1903): pp. 398–400. For additional illustrations of motive power and other equipment, see Middleton, *op. cit.*, pp. 26–35, and Lawrence W. Sagle, *B & O Power* (Medina, O., Alvin W. Staufer, 1964), pp. 310–315.

because of inadequate interior space for transformers, swiching equipment, and train-heating boiler.[24]

The novel feature of the B. and O. locomotives was a method of transmitting the armature torque to the axle without gears by means of what later came to be called a quill drive. In this technique the hollow drum-like armature surrounds a cylindrical sleeve known as a quill that is fitted in turn around the driving-wheel axle but is not in contact with it. At each end of the quill a plate is fixed from which projecting pins are inserted into matching openings in the solid hub of the driving wheel. The armature thus rotates the quill, and the plate at each end drives the wheels. The aim in using this driving technique, which eventually became the common form for heavy-duty service, has always been to protect the armature from damage arising from the shocks caused by uneven track, but this can be fully assured only by a liberal use of cushioning gaskets and by suspending the entire motor and quill assembly from springs mounted on a framework lying in a plane immediately inside the inner faces of the driving wheels. It was all an expensive protective as well as an operating device.

The company generated its own power in a plant specifically built for the new installation near Camden Station, at the west end of the electrified zone. The generating equipment that supplied current to the locomotives was restricted exclusively to the direct-current variety. The Westinghouse company's earlier experiments with alternating-current transmission and motive power were still regarded as untried novelties, and indeed, the rival claims for the two chief systems of the electrical world were to lead to increasingly vehement controversy by the turn of the century. A small alternating-current generator was included in the Baltimore plant to supply power for the numerous electric lights in the tunnels and underneath the bridges.[25] The

original distribution system was the strangest feature of the B. and O. installation, and it proved to be the part of the equipment that had to be most quickly replaced. Power was supplied to locomotives by means of an overhead conductor that consisted of two Z-bars and a 12-inch wide cover plate, the three of wrought iron, arranged to form a slotted box or trough weighing 30 pounds per lineal foot. The hinged trolley on the locomotive terminated in a contact shoe of brass that measured 1 inch by 7 inches in section by 30 inches in length, the individual shoe weghing 25 pounds. The whole arrangement was heavy, cumbersome, expensive, and guaranteed to cause trouble. The sheer weight of the overhead distributor required an elaborate supporting system of truss-frame gantries, trussed brackets on open-web poles of steel, and massive porcelain insulators (some details of this system appear in fig. 5). The conductors were located 22 feet above the top of rail on either side of the center line of the space between adjacent tracks (an unaccountable detail that in itself invited difficulties), except in tunnels, where the conductor was properly located above the center line of the individual track.

The method of operating trains over the Baltimore Belt Railroad was a compromise between steam and electricity that made it impossible to determine the full potentiality of electric traction in either an economic or utilitarian sense. Since the length of electrified line was only 3.75 miles (Camden Station to Waverly interlocking tower), and since the purpose of the installation was to keep the tunnel and surrounding streets free of smoke and exhaust gases, the officers of the railroad concluded that this end could be served by leaving the steam locomotive coupled to the train during the passage through the tunnels, prohibiting the firing of the locomotive, and using the electric power to haul both train and engine upgrade (eastbound) through the tunnel zone. The westbound run through the tunnels being downgrade, it was decided that the road engine could handle the train without generating undesirable quantities of smoke and gases. The results of the first regular operations in the summer of 1895 were ambiguous. The specifications called for a speed of 15 miles per hour with 30 loaded cars on an ascending grade of 0.8 per cent, but the locomotive was unable to exceed 8 miles per hour, apparently because the motor wiring could not carry a current in excess of the 1,500 amperes required for the lower speed (or at any rate, this was thought to be the case). Moreover, it turned out that even the idling steam locomotives discharged excessive gases through the stack.

Precisely what changes the engineers introduced does not appear to have been recorded, but whatever the case, the severe and exhaustive test runs carried out by the company under the direction of Lee H. Parker in September, 1895, provided far more impressive results. In the best performances a single locomotive easily started and smoothly handled a 1,900-ton

---

[24] Physical data of power, weight, and size for the B. and O. locomotives were the following: weight 95 tons; starting tractive force 47,500 pounds; overall dimensions, 34 feet 8 inches in length, 14 feet 3 inches in height, 9 feet 6¼ inches in width; wheel base of each truck, 6 feet 10 inches; diameter of driving wheels (no truck wheels) 62 inches; weight of each motor 25,410 pounds; motor rating 360 horsepower; voltage at trolley 500; motor winding voltage 250; current at maximum tractive force, 2,700 amperes; maximum speed 50 mile per hour; maximum speed at full tractive force, 15 miles per hour; return circuit in running rails. The locomotive wheel arrangement (two four-wheel trucks) is what would now be designated $B + B$. ["Baltimore Belt Line Power Station and Equipment," *Railroad Gazette* 27 (28 June, 1895): p. 424.]

[25] The equipment of the Camden Station plant included the following: 11 boilers rated at 250 horsepower; four Allis-Corliss compound non-condensing engines rated at 750 horsepower, directly connected to four General Electric generators of 500-kilowatt capacity each. Power was generated and distributed at 675 volts, but a small portion of the total output was reduced to 550 volts for shop motors. ["The Baltimore Belt Railroad," *Railroad Gazette* 26 (14 December, 1894): pp. 846-848.]

freight train composed of 44 cars and three dead-head steam locomotives at a constant speed of 12 miles per hour, having placed it in motion with a starting tractive force of 63,000 pounds. This could have been accomplished only by drawing current well in excess of the motor rating. A single locomotive running light was operated through the tunnel at a maximum speed of 61 miles per hour, for what must have been a heady experience to those in the cab. What struck all the qualified observers was the smoothness with which the hauling power was exerted as well as the power itself, and the steady, continuous pull that followed from the constant torque of the direct-current motor as opposed to the intermittent thrust of the reciprocating steam engine.[26] As of the close of 1895, at any rate, the B. and O. experiment appeared to be full of promise, and the potentiality of the new development as well as the way it would go seemed obvious to trained observers like the editors of the *Railroad Gazette*.

Whatever may be the outcome [they wrote] of the use of electric locomotives in the Baltimore tunnel, there is one valuable practical lesson already; there is a possibility of getting any reasonable pull with an electric locomotive. This fact will be impressed on the mind of anyone who sees the machine take hold of 30 cars and start them without using the slack. In the matter of speed, there is nothing about this service that is intended to show how fast electric locomotives can run. . . . It has been said in the press reports that the Baltimore electric locomotive has reached 61 miles an hour. This is quite probable, as there is sufficient power to drive the locomotive and several cars at 100 miles an hour if the motors were all placed in multiple [parallel] instead of series. Speed with electric locomotives is largely a matter of connection of the wiring, and high speeds are generally more feasible and economical than slow speeds with heavy loads.[27]

But the electrification of the Baltimore tunnels, for all the boldness displayed by both the railroad and the manufacturer, was only an awkward first step. By the turn of the century nearly every major feature of the installation had given rise to unforeseen problems and had to be modified or replaced, or it became a matter of controversy that in some cases was not settled for years. The first issue had to do with the driving mechanism, about which questions arose in part as the result of experience derived from electrifications that followed close on the Baltimore program. On this subject everyone had an opinion, and none of the existing techniques was wholly satisfactory. The original model for separate locomotives as opposed to motorized cars, that offered by the City and South London Railway, was the gearless drive in which the armature was fixed rigidly to the driving wheel axle, but this proved defective for standard railroad service for a simple reason. Since the heavy weight of both the armature and the field coils fell entirely on the axle, and since the tight contact of armature and axle prevented the use of springs or any other shock-absorbing device, the shocks arising from frogs, switches, and uneven track not only damaged the delicate armature but the rest of the motor and the axle as well. The B. and O.'s solution, as we have seen, was to adopt the quill, which eventually came to be widely used, but this proved troublesome for a variety of reasons. The introduction of a plate fitted with lugs and the necessary shock-absorbing devices such as rubber cups or springs needlessly complicated the form of the motor, doubled the cost of the fixed armature-and-axle type, and raised the weight-to-horsepower ratio to two or three times that of the geared motor. In operation the separate sleeve, having a clearance of no more than half an inch between axle and quill, was no guarantee of freedom from damage, especially during passage over switches and frogs. In the repair shop other difficulties appeared: in order to reach the armature the entire driving-wheel assembly had to be removed, whereas in the case of geared motors it was possible to repair the armature without disturbing the wheels and axles. Finally, in order to alter the speed of gearless motors it was necessary to rearrange the wiring, but in the geared form the shop crew needed only to replace a gear to alter the ratio and hence the speed. All this was enough to convince the engineers of the B. and O. to adopt a geared drive for their next locomotive purchase in 1903 and to retain it for all subsequent installations (fig. 6).[28]

---

[26] Since the B. and O. tests were the first to be run with electric locomotives in standard rail service, the results are worth recording. There were four series, all carried out in September, 1895, with a dynamometer car borrowed from the Pennsylvania Railroad. First series: train of 18 (?) loaded freight cars and 2 dead-head locomotives, total weight 910 tons; maximum tractive force of electric engine 45,120 pounds, with motors drawing current of 1,750 amperes 38 seconds after start; current consumption rose from 0 to 1,250 amperes in eight seconds (wholly without precedent in previous electrical technology). Second series: train of 22 loaded coal cars, 1 caboose, and 2 dead-head locomotives, total weight 1,068 tons; maximum speed 11.125 miles per hour on 0.8 per cent tunnel grade; average tractive force on grade throughout run 25,000 pounds. Third series: train of 36 loaded cars, 1 caboose, and 3 dead-head locomotives, total weight 1,600 tons; maximum tractive force 45,100 pounds. Fourth series: train of 44 loaded cars and 3 dead-head locomotives, total weight 1,900 tons; maximum tractive force 63,000 pounds; constant speed 12 miles per hour; maximum current drawn during acceleration 2,200 amperes; current drawn at constant speed 1,800 amperes; voltage 625. The special test with an engine running light at 61 miles per hour maximum required a steady current to maintain speed of 144 amperes. ["B. & O. Electric Locomotive," *Railroad Gazette* 27 (8 November, 1895): pp. 735–736; "Testing the B. & O. Electric Locomotive," *loc. cit.* 28 (6 March, 1896): p. 161.]

[27] "The Baltimore Tunnel Electric Locomotive in Service," *Railroad Gazette* 27 (4 October, 1895): p. 657.

[28] The 1903 locomotives were designed exclusively for freight service, with maximum train weight raised to 2,400 tons, and became the subject of an exhaustive operating analysis by J. E. Muhlfeld, the superintendent of motive power for the B. and O. (see below). The railroad installed new power on the Baltimore Belt in 1906, 1910, 1912, 1923, and 1927. The physical characteristics of the locomotives in the 1903–1912 groups were virtually identical with those of 1895, but for the 1923 and 1927 purchases the weight was increased to 120 tons and the tractive force to 60,000 pounds.

More troublesome than locomotive drives was the peculiar distribution system of the Baltimore Belt line. The heavy contact shoe moved with considerable friction through the slot of the overhead conductor, and rough surfaces caused momentary losses of contact accompanied by damaging arcs. The simple and vastly more reliable retractible frame (later called a pantograph) carrying a bow in sliding contact with a single wire was later developed by the Westinghouse company, but the wonder is why the engineers of the B. and O. and General Electric failed to come up with so obvious and useful a device when it was needed. The exhaust gases of locomotives in the tunnels could never be entirely suppressed, and the consequence was that the sulfur oxides in the gases reacted with moisture in the damp atmosphere to form sulfurous and sulfuric acids that severely corroded the conductor. The problem defied solution, and the railroad replaced the entire overhead system with an exposed third rail in 1901 (fig. 7). But locomotive gases combined with electrolytic action subjected the rail to corrosion, so that the company was compelled to replace it with a protected variety. Beyond this there was the additional problem of protecting the public from the electric rail in stations without elevated platforms, a danger that required the emplacement of the rail in continuous box-like troughs with a narrow slot in the upper cover to receive the web of the pick-up shoe. By the time these changes were introduced the controversy over third rail versus overhead distribution had reached acrimonious proportions.

Another problem that soon required attention was the generation of power at the company's Camden Station plant. The intermittent flow of traffic, divided between heavy freight and light passenger trains, and the low direct-current distribution voltage resulted in two undesirable consequences. The system was limited to providing power for only one train passing at a time through the electric zone, and the irregular, sometimes lengthy intervals between trains meant sudden high-peak demands followed by periods of very light current withdrawal. To counteract this extreme inefficiency of usage and to regularize the voltage level a substation for storage batteries was built near the new

FIG. 7. A Baltimore and Ohio train drawn by two electric freight locomotives, 1909. The photograph shows the third-rail installation of 1901. (Smithsonian Institution)

Mount Royal Station, so that some proportion of power generated during inactive periods could be stored against peak demand. In this way 900 kilowatts of capacity were made available for traction purposes, enough for the simultaneous operation of a freight and a passenger train through the tunnels. But as the weight and the number of trains increased, the company's generating capacity was pushed ever closer toward its limit. An investigation begun at the turn of the century revealed what most of the electrical generating industry had come to recognize, namely, that a big central power plant could readily absorb a single high-peak demand because it represented a small proportion of total continuing demand and because the great multitude of separate customers generally meant a sustained high demand except for the inescapable daylight-to-darkness fluctuations. Another universal recognition by 1900 was that high-voltage alternating-current generation and transmission are far superior in efficiency to the low-voltage direct-current form, chiefly through reduction in line losses and lower current requirement for a given power level (the product of potential and current). The answer for the B. and O. was obvious, and in 1909 the company entered into a contract with the Consolidated Gas, Electric Light and Power Company of Baltimore to purchase all power in the form of 13,000-volt, 3-phase, 25-cycle alternating current, which necessitated the construction of a substation for conversion to direct current next to the Mount Royal battery substation. The railroad was beginning to catch up with what had become established practice by that time.[29]

---

[29] The conversion technique rested on the prior invention (1898) of the rotary synchronous converter, a machine that combined a motor and a generator in such a way as to receive alternating current at one end of the motor armature and to discharge direct current at the further end of the commutator-equipped generator. For most of the problems of electrical operation on the B. and O., see J. H. Davis, "The Baltimore and Ohio Electrification," *General Electric Rev.* **17,** 11 (November, 1914): pp. 1083–1089. Polyphase generation, transmission, and distribution were essentially European developments (see Part II of this article).

FIG. 6. Electric freight locomotives of the Baltimore and Ohio Railroad, 1903. (Smithsonian Institution)

The operation of a third-rail system on the B. and O. with locomotives specifically designed for heavy freight service offered opportunities for comparative analysis that had no exact parallel among existing installations in the United States. This investigation was begun in September, 1903, by J. E. Muhlfeld, the railroad's superintendent of motive power, and the results were embodied in an important paper presented before the New York Railroad Club on 16 February, 1906. The electric motive power was a typical freight locomotive of the 1903 group, which was composed of engines designed to be operated in pairs, each unit having a total weight of 90 tons, four motors rated at 200 horsepower, geared drive, and a starting tractive force of 40,000 pounds. The direct operating cost of these locomotives, including maintenance at the engine terminal, for an average of 5,042 miles of service per month, was $0.345 per locomotive mile, of which $0.061 represented electrical and mechanical repairs. The engines performed very capably, but they did so only with a constant run of minor repair problems—wear or breakage of contact shoes; loosening, wear, or breakage of the pinion gears between the armatures and the axle gears; overheating and wear of armature bearings; wear of driving-wheel tires; slippage of drivers with attendant stalling of train and separation of couplers, which proved especially troublesome in wet weather or with tires of unequal size following differential wear or age; and finally, derailments. As a consequence, Muhlfeld was far from convinced that electric traction was appropriate to the movement of freight, and when the B. and O. placed the first Mallet locomotive in American service on 6 January, 1905, he was sure that it was not. "The results . . . obtained from this . . . locomotive . . . ," he said, "cannot be duplicated by other single units of steam, electric or internal combustion locomotives now in use on American raliroads." [30]   There was good reason for this negative view: the steam locomotive was equal in power to the electric, and its operating and maintenance cost, at $0.245 per mile, was little more than two-thirds that of the earlier machine.

The most valuable fruit of Muhlfeld's analysis was the preparation of a set of specifications for heavy-duty electric freight locomotives that constitute a major pioneer document in the history of electric traction. I offer them in full as an essential part of this history.

(1) A fire and collision resisting locomotive construction within the present clearance and weight limits; simple in design; reasonable in first cost; safe, reliable and economical for operation at varying speeds and power; and accessible for inspection, lubrication, cleaning, repairs and for replacement on track in event of derailment of any or all wheels by the ordinary steam locomotive and car methods, without the necessity for the use of a power crane.

(2) A locomotive that can be interchanged or operated over home and foreign tracks, which are suitable for steam locomotive or motor-car equipment.

(3) A locomotive composed of two or more interchangeable sections, each a duplicate of the other, and equipped so that each section may be operated from either end, and independently or jointly, with any number of coupled sections; the operation under any arrangement to be controlled from a single section by one engineer.

(4) The elimination of pilot wheels and the concentration of the entire weight on the driver wheels, with a maximum weight per wheel at the rail of 25,000 lbs.; and an arrangement of driver wheels providing for a short, rigid, and long, flexible wheel base, without excessive end play at axle bearings.

(5) The elimination of armatures from locomotive driver-wheel axles and the transmission of power to driver wheels not less than 60-in. initial diameter without the use of gearing, in a manner that will insure the economical use of current at the motors for starting and running, and eliminate the accumulation of unbalanced pressure at the wheel and rail contacts as well as the independent revolution of one or more pairs when coupled in series which occur as the driver wheels become slightly different in diameter due to ordinary wear of material, when making transmission in current at motors, or when operating on slippery track or over rails, frogs and switches of varying wear, surface, alignment and elevation.

(6) The least weight between the track and the locomotive frame-carrying springs, to minimize the pressure, lateral thrusts and wear at the rail and wheel flanges.

(7) A high center of gravity so that the vibration of the locomotive, due to the variations in surface, alignment, elevation and curvature of track can be absorbed by the weight suspended over the driver springs.

(8) A proper proportion between the electrical, mechanical and dead equipment weight of the locomotive.

(9) Locomotive motors compact, ventilated, cooled, protected from internal damage and mechanical injury, and of ample range of adjustment and capacity to permit of continuous operation at varying or full speed or power without excessive heating of armatures, commutators or field above the temperatures of the surrounding atmosphere. A thin, tough and elastic insulation material, unaffected by humidity or a temperature of 400 degrees F., and having the requisite dielectric strength.

(10) A development of the maximum locomotive power for rapid acceleration and regular working, requiring no transition, as from series to multiple, in the transmission of the current to the motors, and providing for a uniform increase or decrease in tractive power to prevent irregular drawbar stresses.

(11) Suitable pumps to provide compressed air for the locomotive power brake, track sander, bell and signal operation, together with steam train heating device, and the other usual equipment.

(12) Automatic positive devices on the locomotive to insure protection in event of accidental short circuit, or disablement of the engineer.

(13) An arrangement on the locomotive which will automatically provide for electrical breaking (sic) and return to the line for the use of pulling locomotives, a considerable percentage of the energy that is generated by trains descending grades, or stopping, and which energy is ordinarily wasted in destroying material and equipment by brake-shoe action on wheels and rails.

(14) A high potential current producing, and an aerial

---

[30] Quoted in "Large Electric and Steam Locomotive," *Street Railway Jour.* 27, 8 (24 February, 1906): p. 308. The locomotive in question was of the 0–6–6–0 wheel arrangement and developed 74,000 pounds starting tractive force in compound working, and 84,000 pounds as a simple or single-pressure machine.

conveying system, reasonable in first cost and economical for maintenance; the generation of the electrical energy at a central plant for the least cost per kilowatt-hour; the transmission of the lowest current over the minimum amount of metal contained in the overhead contact lines, protected for weather, voltage and lightning conditions, and insuring continuous operation in event of line or equipment failure or accident; the conservative use of battery as storage for extra power that can be generated at small cost during light load and utilized to good advantage during intermittent and peak loads; the least number of transformer or converter stations; the minimum feeder, conversion and resistance losses in current, and the elimination of electrolytic action.[31]

The specifications represented a thoroughgoing prescription for the state of the art at the time, but all of them were to be realized insofar as it was technically possible during the subsequent evolution of electrical traction.

III. BRANCH LINE PROJECTS OF THE NEW HAVEN AND THE PENNSYLVANIA

Two minor programs of electrification were implemented almost simultaneously with that of the Baltimore Belt, and they involved such radically different operating requirements and technical solutions that if nothing else they considerably broadened the horizon of possibilities in electrical traction on steam railroads. The two companies involved in these ventures were the New York, New Haven and Hartford and the Pennsylvania railroads, but the operating priority, which was a matter of weeks, appears to belong to the New Haven. A long-growing complex of traffic and demographic factors underlay the decision to take the first step in what was to be a forerunner to one of the great electrified systems of North America. Through the usual combinations of extension of lines, stock ownership, leases, acquisitions, and mergers the New Haven had by the mid-1890's put together a continuous more or less unified system between New York and Boston which enjoyed a high-density, rapidly increasing traffic in the region bounded by the two cities. Several characteristics of the volume and pattern of this traffic distinguished it from all other rail operations in the United States. First was the fact that the New Haven system embraced a great multitude of branch lines serving communities in Connecticut, Rhode Island, and eastern Massachusetts; more remarkable was the presence of an extraordinarily high traffic density on many of these branches, a volume that the officers of great trunk railroads would have envied on main lines. What further set the road apart from others was the very high proportion of passenger to all traffic, so high throughout its early history, in fact, that the management of the road was contemptuous of freight traffic until the late nineteenth century. It offered no regular freight service until 1852; passenger revenue in 1859 exceeded freight revenue by a ratio of four to one, and

it was not until the decade of the eighties that freight revenues overtook passenger. Even then the phenomenon was temporary, and the rate of growth of passenger revenues for many years exceeded the similar rate for freight by about 60 per cent.[32]

But there were two high prices that a railroad company had to pay for this seemingly utopian state of affairs. One was extremely high terminal charges in relation to over-the-line operating expenses, and such charges included not only the cost of freight and passenger terminals, warehouses, yards, and harbor facilities in the major cities, but also of the numerous engine terminals that multiplied to a staggering degree on high-density branch lines. The other was early and increasing vulnerability to trolley-car competition. The railroad tried to meet the latter in two ways: the first was the outright purchase of competing traction lines continuing to the point where it began to threaten the financial soundness of the company, and the second was the attempt to beat the thorny little competitors at their own game. The mehod was to provide enticingly frequent high-speed service wherever the trolley threatened, not only to regain lost traffic but to attempt to reduce the costs of steam-locomotive operation. There was no question about the threat: a survey conducted by the New Haven in the latter part of 1895 revealed that on fourteen selected branch lines paralleled by newly built trolley lines the loss of traffic from the railroad to the interurban car between 1894 and 1895 ranged from 10 to 88 per cent, with an average loss of 54 per cent.[33] The officers decided to meet the problem head on by establishing electrified operation on various branch lines that would duplicate the trolley competition in quality of service and fares and would thus generate new as well as regain lost traffic where the promise would appear to exist. The program was placed in the charge of N. H. Heft, a self-taught electrical engineer, and between 1894 and 1907 the company completed eleven separate branch-line installations.[34]

The first of these electrifications was another elabo-

---

[31] Ibid., pp. 307–308.

[32] The New Haven's freight revenues in 1859 were $189,144, against passenger revenues of $776,961. In the fifteen years from 1888 to 1903 freight revenues increased from $5,648,184 to $22,953,017, or 306 per cent, while passenger revenues increased from $4,118,370 to $23,926,150 (again higher than freight), or 480 per cent. [Clarence Deming, "The Upbuilding of a Railroad System," Railroad Gazette 36, 19 (6 May, 1904): p. 343.]

[33] Ibid.

[34] Technical details of the New Haven branch line projects may be found in the following sources: N. H. Heft, "Application of Electricity to Railroads Now Operated by Steam Power," Railroad Gazette 29, 44 (29 October, 1897): pp. 763–765, and idem., Street Railway Review 7, 11 (15 November, 1897): pp. 743–750; "The Nantasket Beach Road," Railroad Gazette 27 (2 August, 1895): p. 512; "Steam-Turbine Power Plant of the New York, New Haven and Hartford Railroad at Warren, R. I.," Street Railway Jour. 25, 3 (21 January, 1905): pp. 111–112; "Trolleyizing the Nantasket Beach Railroad," Railroad Gazette 27 (14 June, 1895): pp. 377–378.

FIG. 8. Electric motor car and trailers, New Haven Railroad, Nantasket Beach Branch, 1895. (*Railroad Gazette*)

rate experiment in the new technology, since the chief aim was to test an untried type of motive power in the movement of light-weight trains under a high-density traffic pattern. The choice was the so-called Nantasket Beach Branch, originally extending the 7.2 miles from Nantasket Junction, near Hingham, Massachusetts, to Pemberton, a beach resort on the Atlantic Coast. The initial installation was made in 1894–1895, opening on 14 June of the latter year, and was progressively extended to East Weymouth, Braintree, and Cohasset in 1896–1899. Since the Nantasket branch served almost exclusively a recreational traffic, operations were restricted to the four months of late spring and summer. The short distance, the physical characteristics of the line, and the frequency of the schedules made the Nantasket service little different from an interurban railway operation, and the railroad based its program on experience gained from operating the streetcar lines of Stamford and Meriden, Connecticut. The 10.6-mile double-track from Nantasket Junction to East Weymouth consisted mainly of curves and included fifteen way stations plus the terminals for an average spacing of 0.6 mile between stops. The plan called for the operation of thirty-three trains in each direction per weekday plus an additional four on Sunday to meet the Boston-Pemberton boats. The schedule required that each train cover the 10.6 miles in 26 minutes, including the fifteen intermediate stops, for an average speed of 24.5 miles per hour. The individual train was allowed 4 minutes at the Pemberton dock to discharge passengers, reverse the direction of operation, and take on a new load. This extremely rapid turnover was possible only because of the open summer cars employed as rolling stock that allowed passengers to board at every seat (fig. 8). The fare was fixed at ten cents for the one-way trip, and the schedule aimed at establishing half-hour service from 6 A.M. to 11:30 P.M., which was to continue without interruption seven days a week. As Heft correctly concluded, no steam locomotive could possibly maintain such a schedule because it lacked

adequate accelerating power and the capacity to run continuously for seventeen hours, or any sizable fraction thereof. Trolley-car experience indicated that electric motive power could do so most satisfactorily.

The installation of 1894–1895 included an overhead trolley line and trains made up of a motor car weighing 32 tons and equipped with two 125-horsepower geared motors on the forward truck, wiring for a 600-volt direct-current operation, and a trailer weighing 25 tons, the two cars together having a capacity of 192 passengers (fig. 8). The motor unit was able to accelerate this 57-ton train to 31 miles per hour in the shortest station interval, which was only 1,800 feet. The contact device was the typical rigid trolley pole with the grooved wheel that was nearly universal in American street railway practice. The distribution and transmission wires were supported in a primitive manner by later standards: the former was carried on insulators suspended from iron brackets fixed to wooden poles, but the latter was simply strung over grooved cast-iron caps fixed to the top of the poles, the wooden shaft thought to provide sufficient insulation. The company generated its own power in a plant located adjacent to the Nantasket Beach station and equipped with eight boilers providing steam for two steam engine-generator units rated at 550 kilowatts. The plant apparently never operated at capacity, but the cost of generating power was kept low by the practice of mixing partially burned locomotive cinders (called sparks) with fresh coal. The technique required a forced draft maintained with live steam, which was claimed partially to decompose into its constituent hydrogen and oxygen and thereby raise the temperature of the fire. The result of this model example of fuel conservation was a reduction of 50 per cent in the unit cost of producing power, according to Heft's analysis.[35]

With respect to traffic the Nantasket Beach Branch was at first an impressive success, but passenger volume began to decline in 1901 and fell disastrously when the city of Boston turned the beach area into a public park and the street railway company extended streetcar service into the area in 1904. Traffic on the branch during the summer of 1895 was nearly double what it had been during the previous summer and it more than doubled again by 1897, the rise thereafter being gratifying but somewhat less spectacular. From the technological and financial standpoints, however, the line could hardly be regarded as an unqualified success. The first trouble paralleled the experience of the B. and O. at Baltimore, and indeed it was to harass the street railways down

---

[35] The cost was 0.56¢ per kilowatt-hour with fresh coal only, and 0.28¢ per kilowatt-hour with a mixture of coal and "sparks." Several unanswered questions are involved here: Heft did not give the proportion of coal to cinders, the heat content of the latter, nor the labor of culling them out of the ash and loading them at the engine terminal. [See N. H. Heft, "Application of Electricity to Railroads . . . ," *Street Railway Rev.* **7**, 11 (15 November, 1897): pp. 743–750.]

through the years. The operation of the overhead trolley system was so unsatisfactory as to constitute an outright plague: the trolley wheels were quickly damaged beyond use by arcs arising from the heavy current (as high as 1,000 amperes) and the lack of continuous contact between trolley wheel and wire, and by repeated "jumping of the wire" on curves, a nuisance in itself as well as a source of breakage. As a result, the company turned to a third rail for the East Weymouth extension of 1896 to make a comparative analysis as well as to avoid the previous difficulties. The conducting rail was an inverted V-shaped trough of iron carried on wood blocks doweled to the ties. The shoes rode along the flattened and exposed apex of this trough, being held to the rail simply by gravity and to the truck frame by brittle, easily broken cast-iron links (a deliberate practice to avoid damage to the shoe at an obstruction). Shoes were also fixed to trailer cars in order to maintain a flow of current into the motors while passing over switches and grade crossings. The running rail served as a return in the electrical circuit. The installation was simple, inexpensive, and relatively trouble-free, but the low exposed rail was easily flooded at depressions along the line during heavy showers, with a consequent leakage of current which at a potential of 600 volts could constitute a danger to repairmen and maintenance-of-way gangs as well as a loss of power. The great appeal of the third rail to the company was the comparatively low cost of its installation, which was $3,000 per mile of line as opposed to $6,000 per mile for the overhead trolley. But when either of these figures was added to the cost of constructing the line in the first place, and when the cost of maintaining electrical equipment was added to that of track maintenance, it became obvious to the officers of the railroad that at the very least electrification was a controversial idea. For the first five years of its operation, at any rate, the Nantasket Beach Branch gave a good account of itself: traffic expanded rapidly, the motor cars revealed powers of acceleration far beyond those of a steam locomotive, the on-time record was a cause of congratulation, and the power consumption appeared to be modest.[36]

The question from the beginning was whether operating features and traffic expectations justified the high cost of electrification, and the various pros and cons were nicely balanced by the editor of the *Railroad Gazette* at the very start of the Nantasket Beach operations.

There should be no misunderstanding about the reasons for the conversion. It was not made with any idea of saving on the cost of existing business. In fact, the fixed charges and operating expenses will be greatly increased. It was believed, however, that an entirely new business could be created; and also (and this perhaps was the most important consideration) it was believed that a body of useful knowledge could be gathered which will soon be needed, and which can be applied to the trolleyizing of other portions of the . . . system, and perhaps to branches yet to be built. . . . It is highly probable that an analysis of the situation would show that the passengers now handled, or likely to be handled for a season or two, at any rate, could be taken care of cheaper by trains hauled by light steam locomotives than they can be by the electric equipment; but, on the other hand, an essential element in building up the sort of traffic which it is hoped to create is running single cars frequently, which can be done cheaper by electricity than by steam locomotives, *if they are frequent enough.* A very few elevated railroad locomotives would have done the work done at Nantasket Beach today at a great saving in fixed charges and a considerable saving in working expenses. But the attractions of electricity would not have been *present,* and the experimental demonstration would not have been made.[37]

The essential point in the whole program, as the *Gazette's* editor understood, was that the New Haven, to a far greater degree than the B. and O., was embarked on a technological counterpart of an experiment typical of the physical sciences in the late nineteenth century. The company, accordingly, soon launched into other electrification plans. In 1896–1897 the Hartford-New Britain-Berlin branch in Connecticut was converted to electrical operation with features nearly identical with those of the Nantasket Beach line—motor cars hauling one or two trailers (which were sometimes standard railroad coaches), half-hourly service restricted to the summer months, average speeds of 28 to 31 miles per hour with the maximum at 50, and a 600-volt direct-current distribution system by third rail. The company-owned plant was located at Berlin, and again the fuel was a mixture of fresh coal and locomotive cinders, which reduced the fuel costs to 0.40¢ per kilowatt-hour. The results appeared to justify the investment: between Hartford and New Britain the railroad beat the trolley time by 20 minutes as opposed to 55 minutes and the trolley fare by 10 cents against 15 cents; in similar three-month periods of 1896 and 1897 the traffic increased 400 per cent. The company was so enthusiastic about the prospects of the new form of motive power that it undertook an ambitious program of branch-line electrification in the areas of Hartford and Stamford, Connecticut, and Providence, Rhode

---

[36] Acceleration tests conducted in 1896, for example, yielded the following results:

Train weight (cars plus small freight load)	62 tons
Length of run (Nantasket-Weymouth)	10.6 miles
Number of stops	13
Average distance between stops	4,288 feet
Time of run, start to stop	30 minutes 50 seconds
Average speed	20.6 miles per hour
Maximum speed	42.7 miles per hour
Power consumed per train mile	4.723 kilowatt-hours

The steep rise of the speed curve for any station-to-station run best revealed the unusual accelerating power of the train. (Heft, *op. cit., Railroad Gazette* and *Street Railway Jour.*).

---

[37] "The Working of an Electric Railroad," *Railroad Gazette* 27 (2 August, 1895): p. 517. European experience was in a few years to lead to opposite conclusions with respect to operating costs (see Part II of this article).

FIG. 9. Electric switching locomotive, Manufacturers Railroad. The locomotive was originally built in 1893 and acquired by the railroad company, a New Haven subsidiary, in 1896. The lower photograph shows the motor and driving wheel assembly. (Photo by Industrial Photo Service; courtesy William D. Middleton and Kalmbach Publishing Company)

Island, completing five installations in the period of 1898 to 1907.[38] The operating features of these lines were virtually the same as those in the pioneer installation at Nantasket Beach, the most striking difference being the location of the third rail between the running rails on the Bristol, Connecticut, branch. This oddity led to considerable trouble because of its less noticeable accessibility to trespassers and the widespread fear of the public that electricity supposedly emanating from the exposed rail was a menace to life.

---

[38] The particular branches with their dates of completion were the following: New Britain-Bristol, Connecticut, 1898; Stamford-New Canaan, 1899; Providence-Bristol-Fall River, Rhode Island, 1901; Berlin-Meriden-Cromwell, Connecticut, 1906; East Hartford-Melrose, 1907. (For maps and chronological outline of the electrification of these lines, see Middleton, *op. cit.,* pp. 428–429.)

The success of the electrical operation of passenger trains prompted the New Haven Railroad to widen the scope of its program to include freight service, although the initial step was so modest as to be scarcely noticeable. At New Haven, Connecticut, the company owned jointly with various manufacturers on the line a little switching road known as the Manufacturers Railroad, which provided an industrial switching service on a two-mile track extending from Cedar Hill Junction to the end of a row of waterfront factories lying along a city street. Numerous closely spaced industrial spurs, sharp curves, a short grade of 2.5 per cent, the location of the line on a densely built city street, and the fact that a locomotive would stand idle through much of the day led the railroad to reject steam locomotives in favor of what was probably the last surviving horse-operated railroad in the country. In 1896 the officers of the New Haven decided to make a single leap from the primitive to the most sophisticated: they ordered a small switch engine from the General Electric Company in the same year and thus introduced electrical switching operations into the United States (fig. 9).[39] The locomotive in question had actually been built as an experimental machine in 1893 and had been exhibited at the World's Columbian Exposition in Chicago, where it understandably attracted much attention as the manufacturer's first locomotive product. Weighing 29 tons and exerting a tractive effort of 7,000 pounds, the little four-wheel machine with overhead trolley was very nearly the ideal answer and certainly more reliable than horses. The motors, wound for a current of 600 amperes at a potential of 500 volts, drove the wheels by means of a gearless quill acting through an odd kind of flexible coupling in the form of an iron plate encircling the axle. In order to minimize shocks arising from numerous switches, spurs, and irregularities in the street-laid track the entire motor assembly was mounted on coil springs resting on the inside framework of the truck. The only difficulties arose from the overhead distribution system necessitated by the street track and spurs extending into factory buildings. It was a problem that defied a satisfactory solution as long as the conventional streetcar trolley pole was the standard.

The electrical installation for the Manufacturers Railroad worked well enough for better than half a century (until 1948), and it was one of the many experiments of the New Haven that led some enthusiasts to propose what would have been the grandest electrification program in our pioneer age and the first terminal electrification in the United States. South Station, Boston (1896–1899), for years the busiest rail terminal in the United States, was considered a prime candidate for conversion to electrical operation until the New Haven management, especially the new president, C. S.

---

[39] "An Electric Switching Locomotive," *Railroad Gazette* **29** (8 January, 1897): p. 25.

Mellen, began to have doubts about how this lively new program was working out. As a matter of fact, the financial and operating results had become thoroughly ambiguous by the turn of the century. Summer-only operations clearly proved to be a mistake: the Nantasket line, for example, began to suffer a serious erosion of traffic, losing 24 per cent of its passengers and 40 per cent of its revenues between 1901 and 1902, and a further look at the records indicated that it had seldom earned a profit.[40] The Hartford-New Britain-Bristol line, on the other hand, appeared to offer the most gratifying results: over the three years of 1900–1902 gross revenues were $447,400 against direct operating expenses of $145,223, for an operating ratio of 32 per cent. But the company had never included maintenance-of-way expenses in these calculations and did not seem to know precisely what proportion of such costs should be allocated to the operating expenses of the electrified branch (the figures were apparently recorded on a divisional basis). If the maximum figure for the system of $1,500 per mile of line were added to the operating costs, the ratio would still be a handsome 38.5 per cent. In the case of the most heavily used of these electrified lines—Providence-Bristol, Rhode Island, which carried 4,998,-314 passengers in 1902—the total of operating and maintenance-of-way costs plus fixed charges suggested that the well-patronized branch barely broke even. For the year ended 30 September, 1902, the electrified lines as a group yielded an operating ratio ranging from 67.5 to 76.6 per cent, the figure depending on the choice of $1,000 or $1,500 per mile for maintenance of way costs.

The financial returns were thus either ambiguous or downright discouraging. Some of the technological features, though perhaps suitable to a service little beyond the interurban car variety, were in fact primitive. The overhead trolley system repeatedly broke down as the result of severe arcing, cracked wheels, and snapped trolley lines, along with exigencies imposed by the weather. These experiences reinforced the company's prejudice against overhead systems, an ironic attitude in view of the fact that the New Haven pioneered in the overhead catenary system for heavy-duty, high-speed main line service in its New York area main line electrification of 1907. Profound technological differences, however, lay between the two programs. Although the third rail did away with the problems of trolley operation, many of its features proved to be a nuisance. It had to be interrupted at all switches, rail crossings, and street crossings. In its uncovered state it was sometimes coated with ice in a sleet storm, fre-

quently buried in the commonplace New England snowstorms, or drowned in a sudden shower, and it was everywhere a safety hazard to anyone walking near or upon the line, from veteran trackmen to exuberant children. It was clear that better solutions were necessary, and the railroad company's disillusionment was reflected in early abandonments—portions of the Nantasket Beach Branch in 1904 and the Hartford-Bristol line in 1905, though it is true that the remainder of the electrified family survived until the depression years of 1932–1938.[41]

An electrified installation of short length and shorter life coincided with the New Haven program. On 22 July, 1895, the Pennsylvania Railroad inaugurated electrified service on the branch line between Burlington, New Jersey, on the Delaware River, and Mount Holly, 7.2 miles to the south.[42] It could only be regarded as the least promising experiment in generating traffic on neglected lines in the history of the technique. The prospects were nearly hopeless because both ends of the line, which was once part of the Camden and Amboy Railroad, lay on main lines between the Philadelphia metropolitan area and the central and north Jersey shore. Traffic was consequently restricted to local travel between the two terminal points. The company built new motor cars equipped with a 75-horsepower motor on each axle, the 300-horsepower total designed to handle trains at 50 miles per hour with an overhead trolley for a direct-current distribution system. A ten-cent fare and schedule that called for 18 trains in each direction were insufficient to generate enough traffic to pay all the costs and charges, and when the power plant was destroyed by fire in 1901 the company returned to operation with steam locomotives.

IV. MANUFACTURERS' EXPERIMENTAL LOCOMOTIVES

The electrification programs of the New Haven and the Pennsylvania railroads were so limited in scope and so completely restricted to a single, highly specialized kind of traffic that in retrospect their ultimate value appears to have lain more in experimentation on what to avoid than in how to advance the art. The Baltimore installation, on the other hand, though confined to slow-speed train movements over a very short length of track, contained much greater value for future developments if only because of the heavier demands and the higher level of power necessary to satisfy them. Progress in the new technique lay in the same direction, and important steps came in concentrated form around 1895–1897 through the experimental work of large

[40] The results of the New Haven's analyses of electrical operations were included in the following articles: "The New Haven's Electric Problems," *Railroad Gazette* 36, 3, (15 January, 1904): p. 45; "Returns from Electrified Steam Railroads," *loc. cit.* 35, 7 (13 February, 1903): p. 118; "The Status of the 'Third-Rail System'," *Street Railway Jour.* 24, 14 (1 October, 1904): p. 463.

[41] "New Haven Abandons Third Rail," *Street Railway Jour.* 24, 14 (1 October, 1904): p. 495; "New Haven Abandons Third Rail Between Hartford and Bristol," *loc. cit.* 25, 11 (18 March, 1905): p. 513.

[42] "Electric Motors on the Pennsylvania and the New Haven," *Railroad Gazette* 27 (1 March, 1895): pp. 132–133; "Burlington & Mt. Holly Electric Line," 27 (26 July, 1895): p. 504.

FIG. 10. Electric freight and switching locomotive manufactured by Baldwin-Westinghouse, 1894–1895. (Smithsonian Institution)

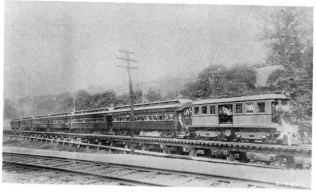

FIG. 11. Baldwin-Westinghouse experimental locomotive, 1895. (Smithsonian Institution, Chaney Collection)

manufacturers and leading inventors, among whom the preeminent figure was once again Frank Julian Sprague. In association with Louis Duncan of the General Electric Company and Cary T. Hutchinson of the Johns Hopkins University he designed a heavy-duty freight and switching locomotive in 1894 that was manufactured in the following year by the Baldwin Locomotive Works, with electrical equipment supplied by the Westinghouse Electric and Manufacturing Company (fig. 10). The total weight of 67 tons was supported on four pairs of driving wheels, each pair carrying a 250-horsepower motor, the four together capable of providing a continuous tractive force at normal operating speed of 10,000 pounds. The high steeple cab suggested switching operations, which were in fact its destiny when it was purchased in the year of its manufacture by the North American Company.[43] Many features were familiar; the novel details were the 800-volt motors and the use of side rods connecting the driving wheels along any one side. Since each axle carried a motor, the rods could only have served some kind of equalizing function. Leo Daft had earlier introduced side rods as part of the primary driving mechanism; both the Daft and Sprague forms were in part forerunners of the so-called jack-shaft drive introduced by the Pennsylvania Railroad for the electrification of its New York terminal in 1910.

The building of the Sprague engine was the first step in the founding of an immensely fruitful partnership in the manufacture of electric locomotives and multiple-unit rolling stock. In July, 1895, the Baldwin and Westinghouse companies established a joint manufacture of electric motive power in which David L. Barnes acted as chief of design and experiment for both companies, and Ernest R. Hill supervised experimental operations for Westinghouse. The first locomotive was produced the same year as a strictly experimental model, though characterized for the most part by familiar elements. The homely box-cab form with open platforms, weighing 84,000 pounds, was carried on two four-wheel

trucks ($B + B$ in the contemporary designation), each axle equipped with a 150-horsepower motor (fig. 11).[44] The locomotive was operated for eleven years (1895–1906) on the test track built for Westinghouse at Turtle Creek, Pennsylvania, by the Pennsylvania Railroad and equipped for operation by either alternating or direct current by means of an overhead trolley system. After prolonged testing the engine was sold in 1906 to the Lackawanna and Wyoming Valley Railroad of Pennsylvania as a direct-current machine. The most important aspect of this initial product of the two manufacturers was the introduction of alternating current as the power supply for the locomotive.

The first group of designs to emerge from the Baldwin-Westinghouse drafting tables in 1896–1897 ranged considerably in weight and power but were identical in wheel arrangement, the box-cab form, and the driving mechanism. The weight varied from 45 to 80 tons (even the maximum was well below the weight of the B. and O. engines), and the motor rating from 100 to 300 horsepower. Since all locomotives were designed with two four-wheel trucks, the total power per unit ranged from 400 to 1,200 horsepower. All motors were the geared type, since the experience at Baltimore had already demonstrated that the quill drive involved an excessively high initial cost, greater difficulties in repairing motor and drive, and a higher weight per horsepower than the geared form. The company claimed, as a matter of fact, that the gearless locomotive would cost three times as much as a steam locomotive of equivalent power. The most innovative feature of the Baldwin-Westinghouse designs was the alternative offered by the manufacturers between direct-current series motors and alternating-current induction motors of the kind invented by Nicola Tesla in 1888 (in the latter type the current in the armature is induced from the current that generates the electromagnetic field).

[43] "The Sprague Electric Locomotive," *Railroad Gazette* 27 (19 April, 1895): p. 251.

[44] "The Baldwin-Westinghouse Electric Locomotive," *Railroad Gazette* 28 (6 March, 1896): pp. 155–157; B. G. Lammé, "Pioneer Electric Railway Work of the Westinghouse Company," *Street Railway Jour.* 24, 15 (8 October, 1904): pp. 542–546.

This invention and its subsequent practical use made the Westinghouse company an early proponent of alternating-current systems for both transmission and distribution.

It was an intimate knowledge of electric motive power rather than extensive railroad practice, which did not in any case exist, that led Sprague in 1895 to outline the conditions under which he thought electrification could compete effectively with steam locomotive operation.

When trains are operated in large units, with comparatively few units between the terminal points, and those at considerable intervals, the steam locomotive will absolutely hold its own. When, however, these larger units are broken up the intervals of train dispatching can be shortened as much as is consistent with satisfactory operation and the number of units distributed over a line made correspondingly large. Then and then only will electricity be used on suburban lines and lines connecting important cities. . . . Electricity will take the place of the steam locomotive only in part, and then only when the number of units operated between terminal points is so large that the resulting economy will pay a reasonable interest on the combined cost of a central station system of conductors and motor equipment, and the traffic existing is commensurate with the needs of such a system. . . . The electric locomotive will fill a [field of its own] to the practical exclusion of all other methods of transmitting energy. It will replace the locomotive on many suburban and branch lines; it will operate almost all street railway systems and elevated and underground roads; it will prove a valuable auxiliary to [general] traffic systems; but it has not sounded the death knell of the locomotive any more than the dynamo has sounded that of the stationary steam engine.[45]

But this is a surprisingly cautious and limited view for a once daring pioneer. There were many other kinds of service and conditions of line for which electrification either offered clear advantages or was a matter of physical necessity—high-density freight traffic; continuous switching in industrial and commercial areas, docks, and interior tracks; heavy traffic in densely built urban areas, terminals, and tunnels; all long tunnels where ventilation is impossible; high-speed long-distance runs. The manufacturers were prepared by 1897 to provide the diversity of motive power necessary to meet these varied requirements. Sprague's view actually represented the conservatism of railroad management, which has consistently served among other factors to allow the American system to fall progressively behind its European and Japanese counterparts over the years.

The editor of the *Railroad Gazette* took a somewhat more imaginative view than Sprague, though equally cautious.

It is quite possible that someday in the distant future a set of conditions may arise which will call for the use of electric motors on main lines running comparatively long distances, as, for instance, between New York and Phila-delphia. There may be a commercial demand for higher speeds than can be realized by steam locomotives. We have not yet reached the limit of speed that can be reached by a steam locomotive, but obviously the boiler and the firebox must set a physical limit somewhere. On the other hand, there is practically no limit to the amount of power that can be poured into a motor from a central station, and so the time may come when special high speed lines may be built between some of the great cities on which electric motors may be used.[46]

The big companies like Westinghouse and General Electric were full of innovative plans, but the American railroad system operated under the great handicaps of pure private ownership unsupported by the resources of the state and of the irrational division into hundreds of small companies mostly lacking adequate capital as well as the capacity to plan integrated programs of improvements. They were unwilling to take further steps until after the turn of the century, and then only in the intensely urbanized area of metropolitan New York. Meanwhile, it was the European engineers who were teaching the important lessons.

PART II: 1897–1905

I. THE GARE D'ORSAY ELECTRIFICATION

As we have seen in the first part of this article, a technological revolution as profound and far-reaching as railroad electrification is a long and complex process, springing from a host of determinants some of which are remote from strictly scientific and technical considerations. It is useful and even necessary for reasons of historical manageability to divide the process into what I have called the primitive, pioneer, and mature phases. This division implies an essential fact, namely, that the pioneer phase is itself characterized by a progressive evolution of such intricacy as to make it difficult to assess the relative importance of the events of which it is composed. One could make a very good case, however, for the construction and electrification of the Gare d'Orsay in Paris as the most decisive event in the pioneer history of electric traction, first, on the basis of the urbanistic, economic, and technical factors involved in it, and second, because of its enormous implications for the future of mass transportation.[1] It was the first electrified railroad terminal, the first such installation planned on a scale adequate to the modern financial and commercial metropolis, and very likely the single most influential work in the design of the New York terminals, one of which remains the largest ever constructed. A great many factors entered into the

---

[45] Frank J. Sprague, originally published in *Engineering Magazine*; quoted in "Hauling Trains by Electricity," *Railroad Gazette* 27 (21 June, 1895): p. 412.

[46] *Ibid.*
[1] The correct designation of this terminal is Gare du Quai d'Orsay, but the shorter form is obviously more convenient and is used as the official name by the Régie Autonome des Transports Parisiens, the organization responsible for the operation of suburban service on the Paris rail system.

Fig. 12.　Gare du Quai d'Orsay, Paris, 1897–1900.
General exterior view. (*Engineering*)

final decision to undertake the Paris project, as we have seen to be the case of the B. and O. at Baltimore.

In the late nineteenth century the various railroad lines that converged on Paris, like their counterparts in the United States and the other nations of western Europe, were experiencing an extremely rapid expansion of freight and passenger traffic. The terminal stations of the city were multiplying, and by the last decade of the century ten of them were in regular operation. They had been planned and built in the pattern they retain to this day, forming a ring roughly centered on the Ile de la Cité and lying within a variable radius of from one and a half to two miles in extent. Within the Paris circuit the main line of the Orléans Railway entered the city from the south along the left (west and south) bank of the Seine River. The company had built three successive terminals at Place Valhubert along the Quai d'Austerlitz, a location that had the merit of lying at the end of a direct line into the city but which was remote from other terminals and a good two miles southeast of the central public, cultural, and commercial areas extending west from the Ile de la Cité.[2] The suburban passenger traffic of the Orléans Railway was growing most rapidly of that of all the Paris lines, yet at the same time the intensive commercial and residential growth of the city was moving toward the west, or downstream with respect to the river, and hence away from the company's terminal. Thus traffic expansion, demographic changes, new traffic possibilities, and the need to reduce the time and difficulties of transferring from one station to another compelled the Orléans directors to plan a new station on a more centrally located site. By the fall of 1897 the officers had made the daring decision to relocate the station a full two miles downstream to the prize site of the Quai d'Orsay; the Chamber of Deputies and the

Senate granted the necessary authorization on 29 November, 1897, and construction began in April of the following year, after the architect, Victor Laloux, and his engineering associates, Brière, de la Brosse, and Sabouret, had completed their plans. The new facility was opened a little more than two years later, in the summer of 1900, to coincide with another of Paris's many expositions.

The site was an admirable choice in its location and by virtue of the fact that it could be readily cleared with a minimum of disruption to the urban fabric, since it was occupied only by the badly deteriorated Quai d'Orsay barracks and the ruined Cour des Comptes, a former government audit office that had been burned during the Commune of 1871. As for its location, it could hardly be improved: lying within a radius of no more than three-quarters of a mile were many of the chief public monuments and civic spaces of Paris, among them the Arc de Triomphe, the Avenue des Champs Elysées from the Arc to the Place de la Concorde, the Place itself, the western portion of the Jardins des Tuileries, the Hôtel des Invalides, the Tour Eiffel, and the Jardins du Trocadéro. The very advantages of the site and its riverfront access route, however, carried with them serious problems for the architect and the engineers. The right of way for the double-track line, 3.2 kilometers (2 miles) in length from the old terminal at the Quai d'Austerlitz to the new one planned at the Quai d'Orsay, lay immediately along the south bank of the Seine through a densely built variety of streets, quays, and other structures which required that four-fifths of its length be placed underground and the remainder in a narrow walled cut hemmed in by river, streets, and buildings. Moreover, the terminal building, surrounded by major achievements of architecture, civic art, and arterial and landscape design, had not only to be a handsome work in its own right but a structure in which all suggestions of trains, tracks, train shed, and working railroad elements had to be suppressed. The solution adopted by Laloux and the engineers was to place the entire complex of terminal tracks underground and to incorporate the train shed together with tracks and platforms within the head house enclosure. The result is a masterful work in the neo-baroque style popular in the Second Empire that did full justice to its splendid river and boulevard setting (fig. 12).[3]

---

[2] The successive terminals of the Orléans line were usually designated as the Gare d'Orléans, but this name was eventually replaced by Gare d'Austerlitz, which is still used for the present way station that occupies the site of the former terminals.

[3] The most readily available sources for the design, construction, and operation of the Gare d'Orsay are the following: Jacques Boyer "The New Terminal of the Orleans Railway at the Quai d'Orsay," *Engineering Magazine* 17, 1 (April, 1899): pp. 57–75; Philip Dawson, "Electrical Equipment of Main Line Railways in Europe," *Street Railway Jour.* 30, 15 (12 October, 1907): pp. 638–643; "Electric Locomotive Used on the Orleans Line in Paris," *loc. cit.* 18, 25 (21 December, 1901): p. 880; "La Nouvelle Gare Terminus de la Compagnie d'Orléans à Paris," *Le Genie Civil* 32, 809 (11 December, 1897): pp. 89–95; 32, 827 (16 April, 1898): pp. 389–394; 35, 887 (10 June, 1899): pp. 85–89; "The Orleans Station in Paris," *Railroad*

The only solution to the problems of underground operation on this scale, carried on in a densely built urban environment characterized by works of the highest aesthetic standards, was an electrified system, which was at first adopted for only a little more than the minimum distance between the original and the new facilities. The approach line was entirely covered for the 2,550 meters between the Pont de Sully and the Quai d'Orsay, and since the rails were to lie along the river nearly at mean water level (an average of five meters below grade), it was necessary to construct concrete enclosures at those places where the line was swung out around abutments to avoid disturbing the existing bridges. All vehicular traffic in the immediate area, as a matter of fact, was maintained throughout the two years of construction. The variety of natural and man-made conditions along this short length of rail line dictated the adoption of four different types of tunnel section: single- and double-track horseshoe sections with shallow inverts, all of masonry; a cut-and-cover length with a roof of narrow concrete vaults springing from longitudinal girders of I-section, the roof supported on walls massive enough to resist the hydrostatic uplift of ground and river water; the broad terminal portion lying in a walled cut measuring 76 meters in overall width by 200 meters in length. The most refractory obstacle along the way was the big La Bièvre sewer, the flow of which had to be diverted and its thick masonry trunk cut through to make way for the rail line. The main problem throughout was the construction of massive walling made thoroughly waterproof to keep the river out of the tunnels.

The design of the station building or head house follows the old and abandoned practice of incorporating the track-platform area within the head house by roofing the area with an immense steel-framed vault opened for interior illumination by large steel and glass skylights. The main floor of the station (equivalent to the second level) embraces two large openings that expose parts of the track-platform area to view from the concourse and service spaces above (fig. 13). This swelling vaulted enclosure is the most impressive feature of the building and offers the visitor the visual drama of the railroad that is necessarily denied us in the exterior elevations. The head house covers fifteen tracks, of which two are reserved exclusively for the switching of cars, and the associated platforms, which are the elevated island type designed to prevent passengers from coming in contact with the electrical equipment (the platform surface stands 85 centimeters above the top of the rail). This was a far superior solution to the wooden platforms flush with the top of the rail that

FIG. 13. Gare du Quai d'Orsay. Interior view showing tracks, third-rail distribution system, and a typical locomotive of the original electrification. (Yale University Art Department)

marked the Baltimore stations and that led to the clumsy expedient of a boxlike enclosure around the third rail (see Part I of this article).[4]

The electrical installation of the Orléans Railway's Paris extension was characterized by sophisticated innovations that had no parallel in American practice at the time, which indeed seemed almost crude by comparison. The full length of the electrified line was four kilometers, the change from steam to electrical motive power or the reverse being made a little above, or upstream, from the Austerlitz station. The power supply was 3-phase 25-cycle alternating current generated and transmitted at 5,500 volts, and thus represented the highest transmission voltage so far adopted and the first use of polyphase transmission for standard rail service. This system was largely rejected by American engineers at the turn of the century, and it would not in any case have been adopted for the short length of the Paris installation were it not for the fact that the Orléans company had already planned to extend the electrified line southward to the suburb of Juvisy (see below).[5] Two substations along the line,

---

Gazette 30, 13 (1 April, 1898): pp. 238–239; F. Paul-Dubois, "Electric Traction in France," Street Railway Jour. 25, 20 (20 May, 1905): pp. 911–915. For the general state of rail electrification at the time of the Gare d'Orsay project, see "Recent Developments in the Traction Field," loc. cit. 18, 14 (5 October, 1901): pp. 489–494.

[4] The extensive open spaces of the Gare d'Orsay, empty in the late night hours, were effectively used as the primary set for the movie The Trial (1962), directed by Orson Welles and based on Kafka's novel of the same title.

[5] When a single coil of the generator armature passes from one field pole to the next the current induced in it reverses direction, and the sine curve that graphically represents one such complete reversal, as well as the reversal itself, is called a cycle. Field coils can be wound in such a way as to cause the armature to generate two or three superimposed cycles separated by a phase interval measured in electrical degrees, 90 degrees in the case of the two-phase and 60 degrees in the case of the three-phase current. (The circumferential distance between two poles is designated as 360 degrees, or an interval of 2π on the abscissa of the sine curve.) Polyphase generation offers much higher transmission efficiency than other forms because

rated at 500 kilowatts each, were equipped with transformers and rotary converters to step the line potential down from 5,500 to 440 volts and to convert the 440-volt alternating current to 600-volt direct current for the locomotive motors. The third-rail distributor was exposed except in stations, where it was covered with protective wooden plates of which the top piece was set high enough above the upper surface of the rail to allow the lower horizontal extension or flange of the shoe (having the form of a channel in vertical section) to penetrate the space between the cover and the rail (fig. 13 shows the locomotive and third rail). In areas of numerous switches and crossovers, like the terminal throat, the third rail took the form of an inverted *T* in section and was elevated above the track, where the stem of the *T* was held between wooden stringers fixed to transverse steel girders. The electrical equipment of the Gare d'Orsay was installed by the Thomson-Houston Company of France, a General Electric subsidiary (see Part I); the locomotive motors were manufactured by the General Electric Company, and the trucks by the American Locomotive Company.[6]

The eight locomotives of the 1900 installation were in many respects similar to the B. and O. engines of 1895 though little more than half their weight. Built in the steeple-cab form, they were carried on two four-wheel trucks with a direct-current motor on each axle rated at 225 horsepower and fitted with a geared drive. The individual unit measured 29 feet 6 inches in length and 11 feet 6 inches in height and weighed only 49.5 tons, all dimensions substantially below those of conventional American power. Restricted to passenger service, they were designed to haul a train of 300 tons weight on an ascending 1.1 per cent grade at a speed sufficient to cover the 2.5 miles between the Austerlitz engine change and the Quai d'Orsay in seven minutes, for an average speed of 21.4 miles per hour. Everything about the Paris installation appears to have worked well enough according to the criteria set down in the specifications, and the only change subsequently introduced was to equip the locomotives with commutating switches that made it possible to place the motors of any one pair (that is, on any one truck) in series or parallel to provide a wider range of efficient speed control. The engines successfully handled a rapidly expanding traffic, which rose from an average of about 125 trains per weekday in 1900 to 175 in 1904, with a maximum of 200 at peak times. Operating and maintenance costs totaled a modest $0.26 per mile in 1903.[7]

The success of the Paris extension prompted a rapid implementation of the company's earlier and tentative plan to extend electrical operations from the Quai d'Austerlitz outward to the suburban community of Juvisy, for an additional distance of 12 miles, or 14.5 miles to the terminal at the Quai d'Orsay. The area south of the city proper was flat terrain and largely unbuilt in 1900, so that the company looked forward to an extensive residential development that would generate a new suburban traffic. This is precisely what occurred, in the now familiar pattern of suburban rail service stimulating suburban growth. Since Juvisy was also located at the intersection of the Orléans Railway with the Grande Ceinture, the chief belt line of the Paris system, the directors of the company expected a substantial increase in freight tonnage. In both cases these hopes were gratifyingly realized, which justified the cost of electrifying the main line and expanding it from two to four tracks to provide separate lines for local and express trains. The Juvisy program was carried out in 1902–1904, and within a year the passenger traffic increased to an average of 200 trains per weekday.[8] The service included both multiple-unit suburban trains and through trains hauled by new electric locomotives that now took over the trains from the steam engines at Juvisy to provide a considerably longer run and hence more efficient use of electric power than was possible on the miniature 2½-mile run from the Quai d'Austerlitz to the Gare d'Orsay. The new locomotives differed from the original models by virtue of their greater weight of 55 tons and their windowed box-cab form which included a baggage compartment within the

of reduced line losses, but its full advantage can be realized only with three-phase alternating-current motors, which still lay in the future (such motors operate at a constant speed and provide maximum simplicity and efficiency with a high uniform torque). American engineers regarded polyphase systems with a feeling bordering on abhorrence. The only apostle of this novelty was the electrical engineer Cary T. Hutchinson, who persuaded the officers of the Great Northern Railway to adopt it for the Cascade Tunnel electrification of 1909. The relative merits and disadvantages of single-phase versus polyphase systems were discussed at length by B. G. Lammé in a paper read before the New York Railroad Club in March, 1906. [See B. G. Lammé, "Alternating Current Electric Systems for Heavy Railway Service," *Street Railway Jour.* 27, 12 (24 March, 1906): pp. 450–462.]

[6] The two companies, their chief manufacturing plants located in Schenectady, New York, had by 1897 entered into the same working agreement as that established by the Westinghouse and the Baldwin firms in 1895 (see Part I of this paper).

[7] Fuel and power consumption for the Orléans extension are given in the following table:

Fuel consumption	3.494 pounds of coal per kilowatt-hour
Energy consumption	5.810 kilowatt-hours per 100 ton-miles
Energy consumption	9.773 kilowatt-hours per train-mile
Operating cost	$0.2555 per train-mile

[F. Paul-Dubois, "Electic Traction in France," *Street Railway Jour.* 25, 20 (20 May, 1905): pp. 911–915.]

[8] For early additions to the electrified lines in the Paris rail system, see the following: "Extension of the Third-Rail System of the Paris-Orleans Railway," *Street Railway Jour.* 24, 6 (6 August, 1904): pp. 176–181; "International Railway Congress," *loc. cit.* 25, 19 (13 May, 1905): p. 876; "New Locomotives and Motor-Cars for the Paris-Orleans Railway," *Railroad Gazette* 37, 17 (7 October, 1904): pp. 419–420; "Notes on Heavy Electric Traction Near Paris," *Street Railway Jour.* 20, 20 (15 November, 1902), pp. 807–810; F. Paul-Dubois, "Electric Traction in France," *loc. cit.* 25, 20 (20 May, 1905): pp. 911–915.

housing. The multiple-unit cars were the kind originally designed by Sprague and manufactured by General Electric. They were equipped with a 125-horsepower motor on each axle of the two four-wheel trucks, the latter being a product of the Baldwin Locomotive Works. The heavy or standard cars were nearly identical with those of the New York elevated lines, but the great difference was the location of all control equipment (rheostats, reversers, relays, and associated switches as well as the controller proper) in the roomy cab rather than under the car frame, where the designers thought it was exposed to too much abrasive and moisture-laden dirt.

The most radical difference between the French and the American equipment was, as we might expect, the low weight of the former. According to a description of the cars recorded in the Proceedings of the International Railway Congress held in spring of 1905, the Orléans Railway operated two classes of trains on the Juvisy run, a light train of 650 seats weighing only 73 tons, and a heavy train of 1,000 seats weighing 286 tons. The exaggerated disparity of the two figures and the extremely low weight of the 650-seat train are puzzling and possibly incorrect. The two kinds of service must have been operated on separate tracks; to fail to do so would have been an invitation to disaster. The Juvisy extension and its much expanded traffic required a six-fold increase in the boiler and generating capacity at the power plant and the addition of two substations roughly at the one-third points along the line. The fuel for the boiler furnaces consisted of coal and partly burned locomotive cinders, like that used on the New Haven Railroad's Nantasket Beach Branch (1895; see Part I), which may have been known to the engineers of the Orléans Railway.

Coincident with the opening of the Gare d'Orsay was the inauguration of experiments by the Western Railway of France looking to the electrification of the line from Paris to Versailles, a distance of eleven miles. The aims of the new program were economy of operation and the elimination of smoke in the numerous tunnels en route. The experimental period of 1900–1901, which included the trial operation of a compressed-air locomotive built like a dummy steam engine, was succeeded by the installation of an electrified system similar to that of the Orléans company. Three-phase 25-cycle alternating current was generated and transmitted at 5,500 volts and converted to 550-volt direct current by means of the usual rotary converters in the two substations. The ten locomotives were actually motor cars with about half the interior space given over to passenger accommodations. They were the product of an international group of manufacturers: the 225-horsepower motors for four of the power units, fitted with a straight geared drive, were supplied by General Electric, but the remaining six, equipped with armature gears that engaged the wheel through plates fixed to the ends of a quill, were a joint development

of the Brown-Boveri Company in Switzerland and the Westinghouse Electric and Manufacturing Company in the United States. These international associations indicate that the early installations in the Paris area were characterized to a great extent by equipment manufactured under American patents, a consequence of the the early dominance of the Sprague, Westinghouse, and General Electric firms.

II. INNOVATIONS AND EXPERIMENTS IN EUROPE

Planning for the construction of the Gare d'Orsay ushered in a prolific period of railroad electrification in various European countries. What is generally regarded as the first inter-city main line to be operated electrically in Europe is the Burgdorf-Thun line of the Swiss railway system, which was converted from steam power in 1898–1899 as the first step in what was eventually to become a system with the highest proportion of electrified mileage of any nation in the world (99.44 per cent in 1974). Switzerland offered both the leading challenge to railroad operations and the most readily available means of generating power in its heavy mountain grades, numerous long tunnels, and enviable hydroelectric potential.[9] The Burgdorf-Thun project was a pioneer example of a rail system operated by high-voltage, three-phase alternating current, but again it was the now celebrated firm of Siemens and Halske that initiated at least the experimental phase of the development. The company built another test track at Gross Lichterfelde, near Berlin, in 1898–1899 to investigate the feasibility of high-voltage distribution as well as transmission, both at a level wholly without precedent in previous railroad practice.[10] The specially built power plant generated 3-phase 50-cycle alternating current at 10,000 volts that was transmitted directly to a three-wire overhead distribution system (two wires for the locomotive current and one for the return, as opposed to the more common two-wire system, which uses one rail for the return). Current was delivered to and from the four-wheel locomotive by means of three trolleys fixed to short posts on the cab roof and terminating in aluminum bows that constituted the much needed first step in getting rid of the troublesome grooved wheels. The interior operating equipment of the locomotive was marked by a variety of innovative features. The high trolley potential was stepped down by means of two transformers to 750

9 On early electrifications in Europe, see Philip Dawson, "Electrical Equipment of Main Line Railways in Europe," *Street Railway Jour.* 30, 15 (12 October, 1907): pp. 638–643. Two later works that survey the whole European field up to the time are the following by Kent T. Healy: "'Battle of the Systems' in European Electrification," *Railway Age* 83, 14 (1 October, 1927): pp. 641–644; "Factors Which Influence Electrification in Europe," *loc. cit.* 83, 4 (23 July, 1927): pp. 142–146.

10 E. Kilburn Scott, "Visit of the Institution of Electrical Engineers to Germany," *Street Railway Jour.* 18, 10 (7 September, 1901): pp. 278–283.

volts for each of the two motors, which had a normal rating of 30 horsepower, sufficient for an operating speed of 60 kilometers per hour (37.5 miles). The current could be delivered to the motor at a maximum of 2,000 volts, however, giving it a rating of 120 horsepower and a locomotive speed of 120 kilometers per hour (75 miles) if track conditions permitted the high rate.

Italy followed close after Switzerland and Germany in the establishment of electrified rail service. In December, 1898, the Mediterranean Railway, a government-controlled company, began experimental service with a battery-powered car between Milano and Monza, a distance of nine miles, and in little more than a year later (1900) inaugurated a similar operation over the twenty-six miles between Bologna and San Felice.[11] But these old-fashioned first steps were quickly superseded by a bold program implemented in 1900–1901 to electrify the steam-operated line between Milano and Porto Ceresio, at a distance of 45.64 miles on Lake Lugano. The person primarily responsible for the decision to turn to the new power and the author of the general plan of operation were in both cases Giuseppe Oliva, director-general of the company. A variety of physiographic and economic factors underlay this decision. The region is characterized by a piedmont topography rising steadily toward the foot of the steeply climbing mountains around the lake. The terrain required a railroad line marked by numerous sharp curves and by grades ranging from 0.153 per cent for the first four miles above the larger city to an average of 1.52 per cent for the last three, with a ruling grade of 2 per cent along the way. But what made for high operating expenses in the movement of trains also offered an abundant source of low-cost power in the rapidly falling Ticino River close to the right of way. Although the company began operations with steam-generated power, it quickly turned to the hydroelectric variety. Perhaps the chief determinants in deciding on electrification, however, were the great density and rapid growth of traffic arising from the intense industrialization of the Milano region and from the heavy excursion travel to the lakes.

The electrical installation, the product of General Electric's Franco-Italian subsidiary, the Compagnie d'Électricité Thomson-Houston de Mediterranée, revealed a number of innovations valuable for the advancement of the art. The steam and later hydroelectric plants generated three-phase alternating current at 12,000 volts, but the severe thunderstorms characteristic of the area suggested the advisability of circuit-breakers rated at 13,000 volts and lightning protection at 15,000, along with duplicate transmission lines for

continued service in the event that one was rendered inoperative by lightning. The five substations of the system reduced the transmission potential to 420 volts alternating current by transformer, then rectified and stepped it up for third-rail distribution to 650 volts direct current by means of the now standard rotary converters. The rolling stock consisted entirely of motor cars that were identical with conventional American interurban cars except for the absence of a pilot. The two four-wheel trucks were equipped with 160-horsepower motors on all axles, the motors and controllers both manufactured by General Electric. The service was easily the best so far offered in speed and frequency: the scheduled time from Milano to Porto Ceresio was 1 hour 15 minutes, for an average speed of 37 miles per hour; in the rush hours the company operated a train every 12 minutes in each direction during a 3-hour period. It was in every respect a success, so that the Italian government quickly took the next steps of electrifying the Valtellina line, along the Addo River near the Swiss border, in 1902, and initiating plans in 1906 for extensive electrification in the Alpine region.

The experience gained from turn-of-the-century electrification in Switzerland, Germany, and Italy, together with the early extended tramways in Britain, provided some data for comparative analyses of the costs of operating steam and electric railway lines, at least on a preliminary basis. The first to carry out a systematic investigation was apparently the British engineer and physicist Carus Wilson, who presented his conclusions in a paper read before the International Engineering Congress held at Glasgow, Scotland, in 1901. His ultimate conclusion, reached after considering all the relevant factors, was that the average total of direct operating expenses of representative steam and electric railways of the time came to $0.237 per train mile for steam roads against $0.0978 per train mile for electric, or 58.7 per cent below the figure for steam operation. The advantage was overwhelming, and it was an important element in stimulating extensive construction and experimentation during the next few years.[12]

III. TESTS OF HIGH-SPEED OPERATION IN GERMANY

The most far-ranging, most widely publicized, most influential, and even sensational high-speed tests of electric motive power specifically designed for experimental purposes were undertaken by the German State Railways on a special track laid over the sixteen miles between Marienfelde and Zossen during the two years of 1901–1903.[13] These costly and valuable tests under-

---

[11] "High Speed Electric Traction between Milan and the Italian Lakes," *Street Railway Jour.* **18**, 5 (3 August, 1901): pp. 137–144. The official title of the railroad company was Società Italiana per la Strada Ferrata del Mediterraneo.

[12] "Electric Traction in Great Britain and Belgium," *Street Railway Jour.* **25**, 19 (13 May, 1905): p. 873.

[13] The most thorough coverage of these tests is in "The Berlin-Zossen High-Speed Tests of 1901," *Street Railway Jour.* **26**, 11 (9 September, 1905): pp. 374–386; further details are in

scored the two great advantages enjoyed by the rail system of Germany that not only made it unique at the time but gave it a clear head start over all its counterparts in other lands. The more obvious was the existence of a unified system that had for the most part been placed under national ownership and operation over the years 1885–1896 under the chancellorship of Otto von Bismarck and his successor, Georg von Caprivi. The other advantage, less apparent but equally valuable, was the close union of theoretical science, technology, and industrial processes in the German economy. The Zossen experiments were sponsored by the national government and conducted by an *ad hoc* manufacturers' association known as the Studiengesellschaft für Elektrische Schnellbahnen. The two locomotives specifically designed for these tests were manufactured by Siemens and Halske and the Allgemeine Elektricitäts-Gesellschaft.

Everything about these engines was unusual if not unique. In external appearance they looked like the traditional steel interurban car of American practice with clerestory roof, ribbon windows, and the like, but the interiors were completely filled with controllers, transformers, cooling devices, air compressors, switches, and wiring, as in any locomotive. The chief differences apparent on immediate inspection were the greater weight and the presence of six-wheel trucks. They were designed to operate at the unprecedented speed of 200 kilometers per hour (125 miles), but it turned out that no existing track would take such a rate for more than a very short distance.[14] Power was generated in the form of 3-phase 50-cycle alternating current at 10,000 volts, a potential that was used for both transmission and distribution, but this was stepped down to 435 volts alternating current by means of transformers placed in the locomotives. (The early runs were made at a 7,250-volt potential, but all equipment was designed for a maximum of 12,000 volts). There were two motors on each truck, the individual motor rated at 250 horsepower under normal operation and 750 horsepower maximum under short-term overloading above the normal current consumption. The driving mechanism was the quill form in which the armature torque was transmitted to the driving wheel by means of a plate having radial arms with circumferential springs at their ends, the whole assembly fitted to a large perforated disc set within the tire of the driving wheel. The rheostat of the controller was made in such a way that the terminals or contact points were immersed in a constantly circulating soda solution to prevent overheating. The presence of the rheostat indicates that control was still effected by means of successive reductions or additions of resistance to the motor current, rather than the more advanced transformer taps introduced with the New Haven's New York area main line electrification of 1907. Deceleration and stopping in the German tests were accomplished by air brakes (manufactured by the Westinghouse company) and by the extremely valuable innovation of dynamic braking, a technique in which the motor, rotating without an incoming armature current, acts as a generator working against the load imposed by the momentum of the train. Dynamic braking was used only at high speeds, when the air-operated brake shoes would be least effective and most quickly worn, so that the air brake was applied only after considerable deceleration. The collecting device was an oddity that was never used again in precisely this form: the three trolley poles rose from short posts on the locomotive roof (as in Siemens's experimental line at Gross Lichterfelde), but the poles terminated in bows set in the vertical plane so as to press against the wire from the side.

The immediate aim of the many test runs was to determine whether it was possible to operate trains regularly at 160 kilometers per hour (100 miles), and whether it was at all feasible to raise the maximum to 200 kilometers. But this aim obviously gave rise to a multitude of questions the reliable answers to which constituted the ultimate purpose of the whole costly enterprise. The questions might be grouped for convenience into three categories: the first had to do with the design, construction, and maintenance of motive power, rolling stock, track, transmission, and distribution, with the continuing concerns being the highest safe speeds and the optimum balancing of all the constituent factors; the second concerned the power consumed at various speeds, the overall power efficiency of high-speed operation, air and train resistance, line losses, the operating costs, and the economic justification thereof; and the third category, stated most directly, involved all questions on how to control and especially to stop the locomotive, such as necessary air pressure, retarding force *per se* and its percentage of train weight, rate of deceleration, and coefficients of friction in braking.

To summarize all the results would require a monograph with copious explanatory notes. The most important conclusion was of course that regular operation at high speeds appeared entirely feasible at costs that could undoubtedly be brought below the level of those involved in the operation of existing steam-powered railroads. The highest speed consistent with safety and comfort proved to be 130 kilometers per hour (81 miles), and the safe and comfortable braking distance for the top speed of 158 kilometers per hour (99 miles) was 1,600 meters (5,248 feet). One haz-

Alexander Siemens, "High Speed Electric Railway Experiments on the Marienfelde-Zossen Line," *Railroad Gazette* 37, 9 (12 August, 1904), pp. 230–234. The motive power is described in "High-Speed Car on the Berlin-Zossen Line," *Street Railway Jour.* 18, 10 (7 September, 1901): pp. 301–302. Marienfelde is in the southern part of the Berlin metropolitan area, and Zossen is sixteen miles to the south on the main line to Dresden.

[14] There were conflicting reports on the maximum speed attained, and two American authorities claimed that the test locomotives reached 130 miles per hour. [See Lewis B. Stillwell, "Electric Traction under Steam-Road Conditions," *Street Railway Jour.* 24, 15 (8 October, 1904): pp. 586–587.]

ard that quickly manifested itself was the poor visibility of semaphore signals even in clear weather, and the dangerously poor visibility in rain and fog. (This problem was progressively solved by high-intensity light signals, cab signals, and automatic stop.) Careful measurements of frontal resistance established the basis for the first scientific theory of streamlining: the optimal front-end shape to minimize resistance proved to be a paraboloid of revolution, but the need to provide space for a cab, coupler, drawbar, and buffer plates required that the form be modified to the segment of a cylinder with its axis in the vertical position. Tests of the effect of high speeds on track led to an important discovery that would never have manifested itself in the slow-speed operation of the B. and O. at Baltimore or with the light-weight motive power of the New Haven branches (see Part I of this article). The rotation of the pins and rods of steam locomotive driving wheels produces an additional unbalanced radial and tangential momentum called a dynamic augment, which must be counterbalanced to prevent destruction of the track (years of constant concern with this problem never produced a satisfactory solution). Under the pure and theoretically perfectly balanced torque of the rotating motor the pounding action does not appear, but another undesirable effect does. The low-set heavy motors, weighing up to 50 per cent of the total locomotive weight, lower the center of gravity of the entire engine to such a point that the massive tangential thrusts occurring at curves, turnouts, and even slight irregularities in the track act close to the rail level and thus cause the rails to spread apart or overturn. It proved to be the thorny problem of electrical operation equivalent to the dynamic imbalance of steam, but it was later solved to a considerable degree by placing the motors above the driving axles. Taken in their totality, the Zossen tests were a model of German thoroughness and the deep-rooted scientific character of German technology. They were essential to further progress in the art, but continued empirical analysis of actual operating conditions was necessary.

IV. PROGRESS IN ENGLAND AND THE UNITED STATES

The investigations were to come mainly from Great Britain, although the privately owned railroads were at first slow to follow up the pioneer South London installation.[15] There were reasons for this reluctance other than British conservatism. The physiographic characteristics of England differ markedly from those of north Italy, Switzerland, and to some extent Germany, and they tended to inhibit early decisions to adopt electrical operation. Much of the land is relatively level coastal plain or is characterized by moderate relief; coal supplies are the most extensive in Europe,

and the streams offer little hydroelectric potential. The country possesses the oldest rail system in the world, and steam locomotives had worked it very effectively. Electricity was felt to be useful only for the sprawling high-density suburban service of metropolitan London and in such other urbanized areas where trolley lines had been extended into suburbs or to neighboring towns. Many of these tramways, as the English called them, were municipal operations carried on at very low fares. Studies made in the early years of the century by various officers indicated that electrified service of the multiple-unit variety offered very striking advantages in meeting trolley competition—doubling of the average speed obtainable with steam locomotives (from 12 or 14 to 25 miles per hour) and clearing of station tracks in as little as two minutes compared to six for steam-drawn trains, the latter a particular advantage in the overloaded stub-end terminals of London.

Ironically enough, however, the initial steps toward realizing these advantages were taken at some distance from the metropolis. The first main-line electrifications in England were opened in 1903 and 1904, the earlier that of the Mersey Railway in the Liverpool area, the later the suburban service offered by the North Eastern Railway between Newcastle and Tynemouth. What was most valuable about these modest beginnings was that they were immediately followed by exhaustive analyses of the comparative costs of steam and electrical operation. They produced the most convincing results assembled up to that time. In the case of the Mersey line, investigations carried on for the first full year of operation (1905) demonstrated that the company could operate more frequent trains at very much higher speed, with a consequent great increase in total train mileage, without an increase in operating or maintenance-of-way costs. In more precise terms, a comparison of operations in 1901 and 1905 revealed that a traffic increase of 166.5 per cent was accompanied by a negligible increase of 3 per cent in operating and maintenance-of-way expenses.[16] For the North Eastern Railway's Newcastle service, a comparison of 1903 with 1905 revealed a reduction in locomotive costs of more

---

[15] "Electric Traction in Great Britain and Belgium," *Street Railway Jour.* 25, 19 (13 May, 1905): pp. 872–874.

[16] The particular operating figures in the Mersey Railway analysis were the following:

	Steam operation 1901	Electrical operation 1905
Locomotive cost per train mile	13.635d	6.290d
Train lighting and cleaning per train mile	1.665d	0.580d
Maintenance and repair of cars per train mile	1.719d	1.075d
Total train miles	311,360	829,898
Total operating cost	£64,662	£69,036
Total maintenance of way cost	£6,055	£3,793

[Philip Dawson, "Electrical Equipment of Main Line Railways in Europe," *Street Railway Jour.* 30, 15 (12 October, 1907): p. 641.]

than 50 per cent (from 14.40*d* per train mile for steam to 6.75*d* per train mile for electricity) accompanied by a gratifying 17 per cent increase in gross earnings in spite of tramway competition. The opening of the electrified line of the London, Brighton and South Coast Railway in 1906 finally brought the new technique to metropolitan London, and the early returns paralleled those of the North Eastern: total operating and maintenance costs for steam locomotives were 15.37*d* per train mile against similar unit costs of 7.52*d* for electric locomotives.[17]

By 1905 railroad electrification was off to a lively start in six European countries (Belgium and Sweden in addition to those we have considered above), and along with it flourished vehement international controversies over alternating versus direct current, transmission and distribution voltage levels, and overhead versus third-rail distribution. In Europe a fairly clear consensus had formed by the middle of the first decade in support of alternating-current transmission, high transmission voltages, and overhead distribution as well as transmission, although England formed an exception with respect to the last technique. The questions of alternating-current motors and single or polyphase currents, however, were far from settled, and there were vigorous proponents on every side. In the United States, on the other hand, the great fundamentals were still matters of continuing controversy, and nothing revealed it better than the fact that the four electrification programs focused on New York City and brought to completion in the years of 1905–1910 presented a mixture of techniques: three used direct-current, third-rail distribution systems, one used single-phase alternating current with an overhead trolley system, but two of the first three depended on three-phase alternating current for transmission.[18]

For all the experimentation of the Baldwin and Westinghouse companies, the manufactured products still tended to be rather conservative in their working details. An addition to the very small number of freight locomotives was one manufactured in 1904 for the Philadelphia and Reading Railroad, for example, which was a little 20-ton machine with 50-horsepower direct-current motors drawing power from a similar distribution current. The one break with the ruling mode in the United States was the overhead trolley, used only because the third rail would have presented unmanageable difficulties for industrial switching (at Cape May,

FIG. 14.   Baldwin-Westinghouse experimental electric locomotive, 1904–1905.   (*Street Railway Journal*)

New Jersey, in this case).[19] The experimental work of the Baldwin-Westinghouse team seemed in 1905 to be even further ahead of American practice than it had been in the late 1890's. The two manufacturers produced a machine in 1904–1905 that clearly stood at the frontier, if not well beyond it as far as actual railroad operations were concerned, even though it was built exclusively for switching on the Westinghouse Interworks Railway. The most striking novelty was that its motors were designed to use single-phase alternating current drawn from an overhead trolley with a potential of 6,600 volts. It consisted of two permanently coupled units each carried on three pairs of driving wheels, the three motors rated at 225 horsepower or a total of 1,500 for the two units (fig. 14).[20] Transformers in the locomotive cab reduced the trolley voltage to a range of 140 to 320 at the motors. With power to spare and a weight of 135 tons, the engine developed a tractive force of 50,000 pounds at 10 miles per hour. Since it was built for switching service, the maximum speed was limited to 30 miles per hour. One seemingly minor innovation opened the way to the advantages of overhead distribution on high-speed main lines: the retractable pantograph equipped with a horizontal bow to collect the current put an end to the seemingly unending troubles of trolley wheels. This oddity was called a diamond-bow trolley in the engineering press of the time.

[17] *Ibid.* These figures indicated the possibility of a rapid amortization of the capital investment, at least in Europe, and presented an entirely different picture from the New Haven Railroad's ambiguous conclusions (see Part I of this article).

[18] I have regarded only the Long Island Railroad electrification as falling within the scope of this paper (see below), since the extensive and heavy-duty systems of the New York Central, New Haven, and Pennsylvania clearly lie beyond the pioneer stage.

[19] "An Electric Freight Locomotive for the Philadelphia and Reading Railroad," *Street Railway Jour.* **24**, 19 (5 November, 1904) : p. 841.

[20] "1500-HP Single-Phase Locomotive," *Street Railway Jour.* **25**, 20 (20 May, 1905) : p. 923; "Single-Phase Locomotive for Heavy Railroad Service," *loc. cit.* **25**, 22 (3 June, 1905) : pp. 999–1001.

V. THE LONG ISLAND ELECTRIFICATION

Both western Europe and the United States had reached the stage where large-scale main-line electrifications were now feasible. I have included, perhaps somewhat arbitrarily, one other program within the pioneer stage, although it is true that the first mature work of terminal electrification on a scale commensurate with modern metropolitan needs was initiated and nearly brought to completion in the same period. The last of the pioneer order was the Atlantic Avenue electrification of the Long Island Railroad; the first of the new was the introduction of electrical operation at Grand Central Terminal. In the very years in which these plans were being implemented a number of the leading participants in the pioneer effort were busy assessing its achievements and pointing out the paths of future developments, their words launched first before the conventions of engineering and railroad societies and published later in the leading technical journals of the time. Some of these assessments we must consider at length, but perhaps the practical accomplishments of the Long Island Railroad take precedence in the order of events, since a long preparation in the spirit of the new scientific enterprise underlay it, and profound urbanistic changes compelled its consideration.

The Long Island program for its Atlantic Avenue trackage in Brooklyn and extensions thereof in Queens Borough represented the first large-scale main-line electrification in the United States designed for an extremely high-density and rapidly expanding traffic, both features that served to carry it at one stroke far beyond the installation of the B. and O. at Baltimore or the New Haven on its various branch lines in the lower New England states.[21] Atlantic Avenue is a major thoroughfare extending roughly in an east-west direction across the upper third of Brooklyn, and for long constituted the chief artery connecting that city with Jamaica to the east. In 1898 Brooklyn became a borough of New York City, and the extensive area encompassing Jamaica from the East River to Jamaica Bay became Queens Borough. The Long Island Railroad, successor

to the Brooklyn and Jamaica Railroad, the original nucleus of the system, built a line progressively westward from a connection with the Jamaica line along the margin of Atlantic Avenue over a distance of 4½ miles from East New York to a terminal at Flatbush Avenue, the distance lying mainly within the city and later Borough of Brooklyn. In 1867 the municipal government granted the railroad company the right to lay tracks in the center of the street. At the time of this grant the community was in major part very lightly populated, regions of customary urban density for the the time existing only along the East River, Upper Bay, and a few arteries such as Flatbush Avenue in the western areas of the city. A great two-mile wide crescent along Jamaica Bay was uninhabited and was to remain only lightly settled up to the turn of the century. When the railroad tracks were relocated to the center of Atlantic Avenue the street lay largely in farmland, and the little steam locomotives hauling infrequent trains were probably regarded as part of the region's bucolic charm. By 1900, however, the street was solidly lined with houses, flat buildings, and neighborhood commercial developments; traffic, as a consequence, had grown to the point where the rail line had to be enclosed in iron fencing with gates at every crossing. This dangerous nuisance led the municipality to pass an ordinance on 18 May, 1897, requiring the removal of the tracks from the surface of Atlantic Avenue, and the New York state legislature in the spring of 1901 belatedly provided the necessary authorization. The railroad engineering department, accordingly, prepared plans in 1901–1902 for varying lengths of elevated and subway line extending over the 30,525 feet from the borough line east of East New York to the Flatbush Avenue terminal. At the same time the company prepared preliminary plans for the extension of the Atlantic Avenue tracks under the East River to a Manhattan terminal at Broadway and Cortlandt Street, but these were rendered obsolete by the extension of the Broadway subway in the opposite direction to Flatbush Avenue and the admission of the Long Island Railroad to Pennsylvania Station in 1910.

The construction of the elevated and subway lines above and below Atlantic Avenue was carried out in 1902–1904 under the direction of the company's engineering department, with Charles M. Jacobs and J. V. Davies as consulting engineers. The tracks were carried on standard steel-girder viaducts above ground and in cut-and-cover subways below, the cuts walled and floored in concrete and roofed by a concrete slab carried on a steel framework. The excavation was carried out in glacial till (mostly sand and gravel with scattered boulders), which proved to be a far simpler task than constructing the rock-carved Manhattan subways. Two features of the new line made steam operation inadmissible, the more obvious being the long underground sections, and the other the repeated changes of grade level requiring connecting grades ranging from 0.70 to 2 per cent. In a densely built urban area the heavy

[21] The magnitude of the Long Island program excited widespread attention in the electrical and railroad industries, with a concomitant outpouring of articles in the engineering press. Chief of the general treatments are the following: "The Atlantic Avenue Improvements of the Long Island Railroad," *Railroad Gazette* 34, 17 (25 April, 1902): pp. 298–300; "Cables in the Long Island Electrification," *Street Railway Jour.* 27, 4 (27 January, 1906), pp. 156–157; "Electricity on Long Island in June," *loc. cit.* 25, 19 (13 May, 1905), p. 894; "The Electrification of the Long Island Railroad," *Engineering Record* 52, 19 (4 November, 1905): pp. 504–506; *idem, Railroad Gazette* 39, 18 (3 November, 1905): pp. 412–415; *idem., Street Railway Jour.* 26, 19 (4 November, 1905): pp. 828–834; O. S. Lyford, Jr., and W. N. Smith, "Problems of Heavy Electric Traction," *Railroad Gazette* 37, 26 (9 December, 1904): pp. 613–617; *idem., Street Railway Jour.* 24, 23 (3 December, 1904): pp. 992–999 (these two articles, though published under identical titles, emphasize different aspects of the subject).

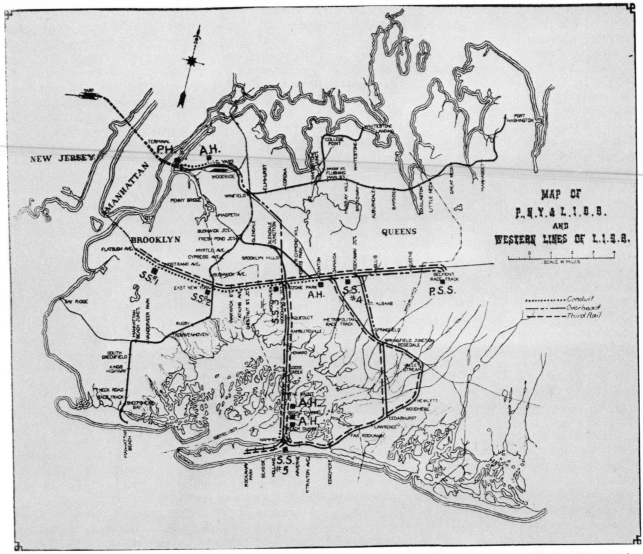

FIG. 15. Map showing the lines of the Long Island Railroad that were electrified in the program of 1903–1905. The map includes the New York extension of the Pennsylvania Railroad and the New York Connecting Railroad. The Pennsylvania, New York and Long Island Railroad was a short-lived construction subsidiary of the Pennsylvania. (*Street Railway Journal*)

smoke and exhaust gases of laboring locomotives were no longer tolerable either above or below ground. The need for electrification was recognized as early as 1900, when the first tentative plans were proposed; these were followed by a long preliminary investigation of high-density electrical operation of the kind provided by rapid transit and interurban service, and finally, by tests carried out in 1903–1904 by the railroad itself. At the same time the railroad's officers had come to recognize the advantages of electrification on other heavy-traffic lines of the Brooklyn-Queens area, so that the program that was ultimately adopted covered the lines from the Flatbush terminal eastward and southward to Jamaica, Valley Stream, Rockaway Park, and Belmont Park Race Track (fig. 15). This ambitious program, unprecedented in its magnitude and cost, was placed under

construction on 15 September, 1903, and completed for regular service on 31 August, 1905.

The preliminary investigation undertaken by the company's engineering staff was another model of the scientific enterprise, but it transcended the usual process of discovery, hypothesizing, and experimental verification in two respects—one, the multitude of variables involved, and the other, the need not simply to determine and to explain the character of natural processes, but to derive predictable, controllable, and reliable man-made processes from the empirical data. In short, the Long Island program provided an impressive example of the unification of the craft and the scientific traditions that had been growing throughout the nineteenth century. Before the work of designing the installation began the railroad analyzed the entire range of its operations in order to discover the precise determinants involved and to establish the optimum characteristics of the new technology. The operational variables could be divided into two classes, external and internal: the former included traffic loads and their distribution, traffic density, number of stops, normal speed, allowable maximum speed for recovering lost time, acceleration rate, layover time at terminals, conditions of track, tunnel clearances, and weather; the latter embraced motive power characteristics for most efficient use, the choice between motor cars alone or motor-trailer combinations, optimum motor size and power, number of axles carrying motors, motor rotational speed, allowable temperature rise, gear ratio if geared drive adopted, truck size, wheel diameter, and allowable weight of power unit. The analysis led to conclusions that can be stated very simply in general terms—optimum weight of rolling stock, construction for maximum safety, the largest truck and the most powerful motor allowable within the tight clearance and weight restrictions—but a host of technical details entered into the creation of the finished product. The specific criteria for the design of motive power and rolling stock were six in number: (1) number of cars per train to vary from one to ten; (2) operations to be carried out predominantly by motor cars for maximum flexibility; (3) optimum size of motor determined by power requirements, clearance restrictions, ease of inspection, and minimization of maintenance costs; (4) maximum operating speed of 55 miles per hour, shown to be the optimum speed with steam locomotives for the greatest efficiency of movement and reliability of service (allowable maximum speed 60 miles per hour); (5) all rolling stock to be identical; (6) all fixed and moving equipment to be designed for a future increase in horsepower of motor.

The railroad company then made a thorough study of test runs carried out on the elevated lines of the Manhattan Rapid Transit Railway, the newly completed subway lines of the Interborough Rapid Transit (1900–1904), and two interurban lines in Michigan, namely, the Detroit, Ypsilanti, Ann Arbor and Jackson and the Grand Rapids, Grand Haven and Muskegon railroads. These tests were supplemented by the theoretical contributions of various electrical engineers and by further experimental runs on the part of the manufacturers: the Westinghouse Electric and Manufacturing Company cooperated with the I. R. T. in various tests, and the General Electric Company operated multi-car tests at its Schenectady, New York, plant. The Long Island then turned to its own resources. The company undertook an extensive series of test runs during the years 1903–1904 involving trains of standard equipment drawn by locomotives assigned to regular passenger service. The primary aim of these tests was to determine all the variables affecting locomotive operation, the nature and extent of their effect, the actual performance of motive power under such variables, and

the kind of electric power needed at least to match and preferably to improve on this performance. If it had done nothing else, this exhaustive inquiry would have been valuable simply for its precise formulation of the character and the range of the variables involved. They could be classified into four categories, which we might designate as train, schedule, track, and external conditions. Under the first were the length and weight of train, the condition of rolling stock, the running order of motive power, and train resistance, which last included inertia on level track, internal mechanical friction, friction between flange and rail (particularly high on curves or under side winds), track resistance, skin friction, and head-end or frontal resistance. The schedule factors were chiefly length and time of run, number of stops, and acceleration requirements, while the track characteristics embraced grades, curves, switches, frogs, uneven rail, and quality of maintenance. External conditions included the presence of grade crossings and junctions, where delays and hazards existed, the taking of sidings for meetings between trains on single track, baggage and express handling facilities at stations, yard facilities, and weather conditions.[22]

The purpose of these tests, as we have indicated, was to provide a secure basis for the design of electric motive power and to institute whatever operating improvements were possible with the new power or were suggested by the tests under any conditions. One originally unintended consequence was the development by the testing staff of theoretical methods or models designed to yield the necessary data for calculating motor size, weight, and horsepower rating, car weight, and proportion of motor cars to trailers. The evaluation of all the data derived from the experimental runs led to the adoption of 200-horsepower motors, one to each axle of the forward truck on the motor car, multiple-unit motor cars with an assumed maximum weight at rush-hour load of 88,000 pounds each, and trailer cars with a weight under similar conditions of 66,000 pounds. The proportion of motor to trailer units was fixed at 3:2 or as close thereto as possible for trains of seven cars or less, and 5:3 for trains of eight cars or more. A total of 130 motor cars was ordered for the initial range of operations in 1905 (fig. 16). They were steel cars, similar to those adopted by the I. R. T., designed by George C. Gibbs, chief engineer of electric traction for the Pennsylvania Railroad (controlling company of the Long Island since 1900), and jointly manufactured by the American Car and Foundry Company (bodies and frames), the Baldwin Locomotive Works (trucks), and the Westinghouse Electric and Manufacturing Company (all electrical equipment and air brakes). The unloaded weight was 83,000 pounds and the maximum speed 55 miles per hour, with an acceleration rate suf-

---

[22] An exhaustive summary of the tests and their results may be found in Lyford and Smith, *op. cit.*, *Street Railway Jour.* **24**, 23 (3 December, 1904): pp. 992–999.

ficient to maintain an average speed of 25 miles per hour with stations spaced from one to six miles. The cars were designed for use in the existing and projected Manhattan subways and were hence subject to the same clearance limits.[23] Cars were serviced at the company's shops located near Springfield on the Valley Stream line and repaired at the larger facilities in Morris Park. Inspection of all operating and running equipment in the cars was made at 800-mile intervals, and general servicing (chiefly oiling of wearing surfaces) every 4,800 miles. Experience gained during the first year of operation revealed that brake shoes had to be replaced every 4,700 miles in local service and every 6,500 miles in express.

All essential details of the Long Island Railroad's electric plant—transmission and distribution systems, type of current, and voltage levels—had to conform to the equivalent elements of the Pennsylvania's installation for its New York terminal, which was then under construction, since the Long Island was to be a tenant in that station. As a consequence, the smaller road adopted 11,000-volt 3-phase alternating current for transmission, which was rectified and reduced to 600-volt direct current for the third-rail distribution system. The generating station was located at Hunter's Point in the part of Queens Borough known as Long Island City and was designed to supply all the power requirements of both the Long Island and the Pennsylvania railroads (fig. 17). The transmission lines were for the most part carried on steel poles along the railroad right of way, but in certain areas they were located in underground conduits. Submarine cables had to be installed at the drawbridges over the inter-island channels of Jamacia Bay (Rockaway Park line, subsequently sold to the New York City Transit Authority), and various lengths of conduit in Long Island City had to be laid below mean high tide, necessitating their emplacement in a tile drainage enclosure equipped with sumps and automatically controlled, electrically operated pumps.

Rectifying and transforming equipment was located in five fixed and two portable substations distributed at roughly equal distances over the electrified lines. The distribution of the substations was calculated in the same scientific spirit as the rest of the installation. The primary station was established at Woodhaven Junction, the focal point of the electrified system, located at the intersection of the Atlantic Avenue-Belmont and the Rockaway Park lines. The other four stations were spaced at an average distance of 4.95 miles from Woodhaven, the minimum distance being 3.2 miles and the maximum seven. Their total installed capacity in 1905

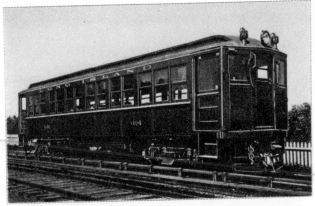

FIG. 16. Multiple-unit electric car of the Long Island Railroad, 1905. (*Street Railway Journal*)

(14,500 kilowatts for the converters and 16,200 kilowatts for the transformers) was based on a detailed analysis of total normal traffic, peak traffic, and traffic density. The third rail was the top-contact or over-running type and was protected from snow and sleet by wood sheathing above the top surface and along the outer side.[24] The design of the Long Island's electrical system was carried out under the direction of George C. Gibbs, and construction work was done under the supervision of George B. Caldwell. The consulting engineers to the whole project were Westinghouse, Church, Kerr and Company, of which Gibbs was a vice-president and Caldwell a member of the engineering staff.

The character of the Long Island traffic placed heavy and even unique demands on the new electrical system. The company's western terminals prior to the opening of Pennsylvania Station in 1910 were located at Hunter's Point (Long Island City) in Queens and Flatbush Avenue in Brooklyn, where the Long Island connected with the Brooklyn Rapid Transit and eventually with the I. R. T. on Manhattan Island by means of the projected Battery-Brooklyn subway tunnel (fig. 15).[25] The heaviest traffic thus flowed over the Atlantic Avenue line, which carried through traffic to and from both shores of Long Island, local traffic between Flatbush Avenue and Jamaica, and intermittent excursion, holiday, and week-end traffic to Rockaway Beach, and Metropolitan, Aqueduct Park, and Belmont Park race tracks. Although the passenger volume on the outlying portions of the branches was insufficient to justify the cost of electrification in 1904, it would have

[23] W. N. Smith, "The Electric Car Equipment of the Long Island Railroad," *Street Railway Jour.* 28, 6 (11 August, 1906): pp. 216–226, and 28, 7 (18 August, 1906): pp. 250–260. Rolling stock installed in 1905 included the following: 130 steel motor cars; 55 wood-sheathed trailers; 5 express cars, and 1 rotary plow.

[24] "Power Transmission Line and Third Rail System of the Long Island Railroad," *Railroad Gazette* 40, 23 (8 June, 1906): pp. 570–572; W. N. Smith, "The Power Transmission Line and Third-Rail System of the Long Island Railroad," *Street Railway Jour.* 27, 23 (9 June, 1906): pp. 895–896, and 27, 24 (16 June, 1906): pp. 936–945; W. N. Smith, "The Rotary Converter Sub-Stations of the Long Island Railroad," *Street Railway Jour.* 27, 25 (23 June, 1906): pp. 968–983.

[25] The newly reconstructed terminal at Long Island City is described in "Passenger Terminal at Long Island City," *Railroad Gazette* 37, 9 (12 August, 1904): pp. 228–229.

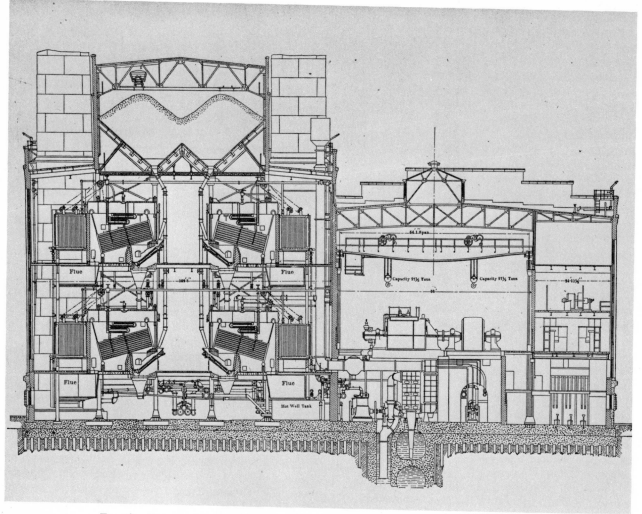

FIG. 17.   Transverse section of the Hunter's Point power plant of the Pennsylvania and
Long Island railroads, 1905. (*Street Railway Journal*)

been intolerably burdensome to operate a mixture of electric and steam-powered trains in this region of high-density traffic and highly diversified scheduling. The feature that required special consideration in the design of the whole installation was the high peak demand that occurred on weekends during the summer beach and racing seasons.   This reached such a level in 1905 as to require the operation of fifteen six-car trains per hour in each direction at various times during the day between Flatbush Avenue and Belmont Park, three six-car trains per hour each way between Flatbush Avenue and Rockaway Park, and two four-car trains per hour each direction between Hammel and Valley Stream, or a total of forty trains per hour at certain weekend hours.   Another factor enlarging peak de- mands was the use of a portion of the Rockaway Beach line by trains of the Brooklyn Rapid Transit under a trackage-rights agreement, the lighter trains of the rapid transit individually drawing less power but off- setting it by the increased density of traffic.   This heavy

concentration of special trains scattered through certain hours of the week, along with projections of future traffic, was a major determinant in establishing the capacity and the distribution of fixed substations and the location of the two portable substations (Belmont Park and Springfield Junction).   Projections of the future expansion in passenger volume proved none too generous, but the railroad was comfortably operating 194 trains per weekday in 1906 on its electrified lines, and the running time between Flatbush Avenue and Jamaica, for example, had been reduced from 35 to 20 minutes.[26]

The analysis of normal operation together with con- tinued special test runs in the period immediately fol- lowing the inauguration of electrical operations gave the officers of the Long Island Railroad ample ground

[26] "Long Island's New Train Schedule—The Part Played by Electricity," *Street Railway Jour.* 27, 19 (12 May, 1906): p. 774.

for confidence in the expensive new system, while the problems turned out to be surprisingly few. Electrification was expected to improve on the hauling of trains by steam locomotives through better adhesion and more rapid acceleration of multiple-unit trains, greater efficiency of motive power and its utilization, and improved mechanical action of all moving elements. The advantages conferred by the new form of power were extended by means of a great number of external improvements—elimination of grade crossings, replacement of junctions at grade by the fly-over variety, expansion of yards, improved automatic signaling, segregation of baggage, mail, and express in special trains, and improvement of the facilities for handling such traffic. Test runs were conducted in 1905–1906 to determine the acceleration rate of multiple-unit power, and the results justified expectations. A three-car train weighing 82,138 pounds per car, or a total of 123.2 tons, reached a speed of 38 miles per hour in 70 seconds, drawing a maximum current of 1,400 amperes at 10 miles per hour. This was a striking improvement over the performance of a similar train drawn by a steam locomotive, which raised the total weight of the train to 171.9 tons. The superiority of the electric power proved to be the case in every comparative test, the length of run in all tests having been fixed by the distance between stops in regular suburban service.

All devices designed to protect electrical equipment from damage or operating difficulties arising from the weather proved effective except for the partly exposed third rail. The sides and base of the rail suffered considerable corrosion during the first year of electrical operations as a result of simple oxidation and other reactions from acid-bearing moisture. The rust was removed by the homely technique of wire-brushing, and the cleaned surfaces were coated with crude petroleum, a sticky substance that picked up dust to form a nearly impervious coating. Snow and ice proved to be a different problem, and one may reasonably raise the question whether the railroad company ever solved it. Ordinary snow or sleet storms offered no serious obstacles to the movement of trains over most of the trackage and under normal operating procedures, but there were combinations of circumstances that required hand-to-hand combat with the weather, so to speak. Trains of one or two cars carried too few contact shoes to abrade or melt the ice that formed from sleet or the melting and refreezing of snow, and the light shoe pressure of fifteen pounds often allowed the shoe to ride up over heavy snow. In stations the snow packed between the third rail and the station platform, causing short trains to stall, and in severe storms bringing a snowfall of twelve inches or more long sections of line were sometimes immobilized until the plow could be dispatched to clear them. These hazards were partly offset through the use of winter contact shoes with cutting edges and a spring-operated device that raised the shoe pressure to 100 pounds, but beyond these the

road simply paid the price for operation with an over-running, partly exposed third rail.[27]

The Long Island Railroad took two more steps at the time of its Brooklyn-Queens electrification program to advance the state of the art. In 1904 the company acquired a five-mile interurban railroad that joined Sea Cliff and Glen Cove with steamboat landings at Hempstead Harbor, an embayment of Long Island Sound. This line was originally operated by direct current, but in the year following the purchase the larger road tied the smaller transmission system to the Hunter's Point plant and thus converted it to single-phase alternating current for car motors as well as transmission. The potential level of the latter was by necessity fixed at 11,000 volts, which was stepped down by transformers in the substation at Glen Cove but not rectified. The two 50-horsepower motors on each of the cars were thus powered by single-phase alternating current, for what must have been the pioneer installation on a standard railroad, although it had previously been used on other interurban lines, which the Glen Cove branch in fact was.[28] The second step marked the expansion of the Long Island's operations to include freight service as well as passenger, mail, and express. In 1906 the company bought a freight locomotive manufactured the previous year by the Westinghouse company, for use in the Brooklyn freight yards and their connecting tracks. The engine was carried on two four-wheel trucks and hence represented a development from the first Baldwin-Westinghouse experimental locomotives of 1895 (see Part I of this article).[29]

The Long Island program represented an essential and major step in the evolution of heavy-duty main-line electrification, although it was confined to the characteristic service of rapid transit in a well-built metropolitan area, however much the regions contiguous to Jamaica Bay might have seemed like uninhabited country at the turn of the century. A similar installation involving more distantly spaced terminals in central New Jersey embodied progressive innovations that offered useful lessons for the Pennsylvania Railroad's New York extension. The West Jersey and Seashore Railroad, controlled by the Pennsylvania and constituting the latter's Camden-Atlantic City line, embarked on the electrification of its entire mileage early in 1905 and inaugurated the new service on 18 September, 1906. The aim of the parent company was to increase the speed and frequency of the West Jersey passenger service and to improve its

---

[27] The engineers of the New York Central and Hudson River Railroad partly solved the problem of buried or coated third rail by developing a thoroughly protected *under-running* rail for the Grand Central Terminal electrification of 1905–1906, which I have regarded as lying in the mature rather than the pioneer phase of electric rail operations.

[28] "A Long Island Single-Phase Railway," *Engineering Record* 52, 26 (23 December, 1905) : p. 271.

[29] "Long Island Electric Locomotive," *Street Railway Jour.* 27, 8 (24 February, 1906) : p. 323.

comfort and cleanliness to the point where it could gain the upper hand in the strenuous competition with the parallel line of the Philadelphia and Reading Railroad between the same terminals. The West Jersey program embraced the sixty-four-mile double-track main line and the ten-mile single-track branch to Millville, New Jersey. The rolling stock and fixed equipment were manufactured and installed by the General Electric Company under the direction of George C. Gibbs. In most respects the Atlantic City installation was a straightforward multiple-unit operation with a coal-fired central power plant, eight substations equipped with rotary converters, third-rail distribution except for an overhead trolley on the Millville branch and in an area of numerous street crossings in Camden, and moderate density of traffic, but there were certain novel features embodying unusual technical details.[30]

The most striking departure from contemporary practice was the transmission potential of 33,000 volts for single-phase alternating current, which was reduced to 650-volt direct current for the distribution system in the most highly automated substations so far designed (the aim was to achieve one-man operation). The high transmission voltage necessitated elaborate precautions to protect linemen working on the high-tension wires and thus led to a valuable pioneer safety device. Power was cut off in the section of the line under repair by the substation operator under written orders from the switchboard operator at the power plant. The former then placed a warning tag on the board, which could not be removed nor could the current be restored without a properly signed order from the central station. As an additional precaution, linemen were equipped with a grounding device joining the transmission line to one of the running rails. The high transmission voltage looked to the future, but the wood-sheathed motor cars carrying a 200-horsepower motor on every axle seemed rather primitive, if not downright controversial. Some of the leading proponents of electrification, among them George Westinghouse himself, warned of the dangers consequent to a short-circuit of the third rail, dangers that might be magnified to disaster proportions with wood-sheathed rolling stock or in the narrow confines of a tunnel.[31] Another questionable feature of the West

Jersey system was the sand-ballasted roadbed, offering an easily drained line at low cost, to be sure, but at the same time posing a serious problem in lubricating journals and motor bearings. Trains were operated over the 64.6 miles from Camden to Atlantic City in $1\frac{1}{2}$ hours, with two to five intermediate stops, for a creditable average speed of 43.1 miles per hour and a maximum of 60. The traffic appeared to have justified the Pennsylvania's expectations: in the first year of operations the West Jersey and Seashore operated 106 trains per weekday between Camden and various points on the main line and another 30 on the Millville branch. The original equipment survived until the depression of the 1930's, when the Pennsylvania began a piecemeal abandonment of electric power that ended with total reversion to steam operation in 1949, to mark another step backward in American transportation history.

VI. POTENTIALITIES: ENGINEERING CONCLUSIONS OF 1905

The experiences gained in the large-scale electrification programs of the Orléans Railway in Paris and the Long Island in New York City offered a reliable guide to all future developments in the field with respect to the design of motive power, rolling stock, and fixed equipment, the methods of constructing or installing such equipment, the operation, servicing, and maintenance of trains, the repair of cars and locomotives, the training of employees, and the use of devices of protection against the controlled and uncontrolled movements of electricity. The inventory of essential elements for electrical operation was impressive in itself and evidence of the rapid technological progress that had occurred in the decade that separated the B. and O.'s installation at Baltimore from that of the Long Island. The new form of traction was technologically impressive to engineers and the results of its use most gratifying to the public, but the total cost gave the whole enterprise an almost horrifying aspect to the directors of financially uneasy railroads (a high proportion in the disordered and fragmented market economy of the United States).[32] The only elements of steam-

---

[30] "The Distribution and Sub-Station System of the West Jersey & Seashore Railroad," *Street Railway Jour.* 30, 15 (12 October, 1907): pp. 618–622; "The Electrical Equipment of the West Jersey & Seashore Branch of the Pennsylvania Railroad," *loc. cit.* 28, 19 (10 November, 1906), pp. 928–946; "Maintenance of Electric Rolling Stock, West Jersey & Seashore Railroad," *loc. cit.* 30, 15 (12 October, 1907): pp. 623–628; "The Power Station Practice of the West Jersey & Seashore Railroad," *loc. cit.* 30, 15 (12 October, 1907): pp. 615–617; "Rolling Stock for the West Jersey & Seashore Division of the Pennsylvania Railroad," *loc. cit.* 28, 9 (1 September, 1906): pp. 348–349.

[31] This controversy reached a vigorous level in the engineering press following the notorious and, indeed, epoch-making accident in the Park Avenue Tunnel, New York City, on 8 January, 1902, when New Haven and New York and Harlem trains were in-

volved in a rear-end collision. See, for example, George Westinghouse, "Concerning Some Dangers from Electric Traction," *Railroad Gazette* 34, 2 (17 January, 1902): p. 33.

[32] A brief recapitulation of the inventory of essential elements provides a useful summary of the technological accomplishments to 1905 and suggests the magnitude of the cost:

Power plant with boilers (including furnaces, turbines, generators, coal- and ash-handling equipment, control and recording devices)
Substations with converters and transformers
Track with suitably bonded joints
Third rail with supports, protection, and insulation
Trolley with carrying wire and insulation
Transmission lines, overhead
Support poles of wood or steel with brackets and insulators
Transmission lines, underground conduit

railroad operation that could be traded for this expensive shopping list were coaling stations, ash-handling facilities, and water-supply systems. The electrified railroad, however, offered social, urbanistic, economic, and operational benefits that far outweighed the admittedly staggering capital investment.

There were many constantly growing advantages, several of them already well known, others being discovered with each progressive step in the art, and there were a number of authorities, some of whom had participated extensively in the creative work of the early years, who in 1904–1905 were providing balanced assessments of the previous achievements and the future possibilities.[33] The benefits conferred by electrification could be divided into three categories that might be most simply designated as operational or technological, economic, and ecological, the last an elastic term useful for covering everything from the comfort of passengers to the conservation of energy and environmental resources.

The first category involved a direct comparison between the performances of steam and electric locomotives in the actual work of pulling trains. The former, given enough weight and the capacity to generate sufficient steam (as in the case of the Mallet locomotive; see Part I), could handle any tonnage that was im-

----

Subaqueous cables
Access tunnels and manholes
Drainage lines with sumps and sump-pumps
Lightning arresters and grounding devices
Insulating elements, power plant, substation, and miscellaneous
Circuit breakers
Switches in countless number at very point of control
Steel frames for wire concentrations at switchyards, cable terminals, and junction points

Some of these elements, most notably generators and motors, are composed of a great multitude of separate, delicate, intricately connected parts requiring great skill to manufacture and repair. A reliable and easily consulted encyclopaedia of electrical technology was a matter of urgency, and it came two years after the inauguration of electrical service on the Long Island: Frank F. Fowle, editor, *Standard Handbook for Electrical Engineers* (first ed., New York, McGraw Publishing Company, 1907).

[33] The most important critical and evaluatory papers of the time are the following: Bion J. Arnold, "The Application of Electricity to Steam Railroads," *Railroad Gazette* 37, 17 (7 October, 1904): pp. 414–415; Louis Duncan, "The Substitution of Electricity for Steam in Railroad Practice," *loc. cit.* 39, 1 (5 July, 1905): pp. 444–446; "Electric Traction in America," *Street Railway Jour.* 25, 19 (13 May, 1905): p. 874; W. B. Potter, "Developments in Electric Traction," *loc. cit.* 25, 4 (28 January, 1905): pp. 154–158; Lewis B. Stillwell, "Electric Traction Under Steam-Road Conditions," *loc. cit.* 24, 15 (8 October, 1904): pp. 586–587; Clement F. Street, "Electricity on Steam Railroads," *loc. cit.* 25, 21 (27 May, 1905): pp. 944–950; J. G. White, *et al.*, "The Substitution of Electricity for Steam as a Motive Power," *loc. cit.* 24, 18 (29 October, 1904): pp. 799–802. A survey written late enough to include the results of the New Haven and New York Central programs at New York is L. R. Pomeroy, "The Electrification of Trunk Lines," *Amer. Engineer and Railroad Jour.* 84, 2 (February, 1910): pp. 41–46.

posed upon the railroad at the time, but a single engine could not do so on every grade, and it suffered an inherent handicap in performing the very service it was called upon to provide. In steam power the tractive force drops rapidly as the speed increases because the locomotive cannot generate steam at a rate sufficient to utilize the tractive potential available from the steam pressure at the piston, the cubic capacity of the cylinder, and the weight on the driving wheels. An electric locomotive, on the other hand, has for practical purposes an unlimited source of power continuously supplying the motor regardless of the speed, so that maximum tractive force may theoretically be maintained at the speeds for which it was designed to operate. In actual practice this is not strictly true, but the decline in tractive effort is small compared to the same characteristic for steam power. Moreover, as we have seen earlier, electric power in the purely rotational motor is used to maintain a continuously increasing and smoothly acting torque, whereas in the reciprocating motion of the piston power is not being continuously translated into continuous mechanical work because some portion of the piston action is involved in exhausting the cylinder. Finally, heat losses from radiation through the firebox walls, boiler jacketing, cylinder walls, and supply pipes, coupled with incomplete combustion of fuel, drastically reduce the thermal efficiency of a steam locomotive, which made it the largest consumer of energy per passenger mile other than the airplane (9,700 B.T.U.'s per passenger mile in both cases according to analyses undertaken in 1973).

The fact that a steam locomotive is a prime mover seems to confer a certain advantage, but in actual practice it does not. It was as much tied to coaling stations and water tanks as the electric locomotive is to trolleys and third rails.[34] The truth of the matter is that the central generation of power, its transmisson at very high voltages over many miles of line, and its distribution to locomotives at appropriately high voltages, preferably as alternating current throughout the system, offers an economy and efficiency of power utilization that makes prime movers such as steam and diesel-electric locomotives, automobiles, and airplanes seem primitive by comparison. What all this means for operating practice is that the higher the density of traffic measured in number of passengers and number and weight of trains per unit of time, the more efficient the conduct of rail service, whereas the opposite is

----

[34] Something of the peculiar handicap of steam power in this respect may be gathered from the fact that the longest non-stop steam locomotive run in the United States was the 177 miles on the New York Central Railroad between Buffalo and Collinwood, Ohio (the location of service facilities in the Cleveland metropolitan area). But this once spectacular performance was achieved only with motive power that represented the highest levels of mechanical design and with the use of track pans, the most expensive way of wasting water while attempting to fill a tender tank.

true in the use of steam locomotives. Central generation offered another and strictly economic advantage to the railroad company that the trained observer was quick to see in the early years of the century, as electrification was beginning to realize its immense potentiality. The steam locomotive exacted high fixed maintenance costs and an intolerable waste of fuel when idling, with the consequence that steam operation involved high irreducible costs, so that in 1905–1907 trains earning less than $0.40 per mile operated at a loss. But since the electric locomotive uses only the power required to move the weight in tow while it is moving, trains for light traffic could be reduced to single cars operating at a cost of $0.10 per mile. These advantages could be most fully realized, as the railroad officers later learned during the replacement of steam with diesel-electric power, only through conversion of entire engine districts and of all types of traffic to electric power; otherwise, the maintenance of duplicate facilities involved the company in the high costs of both forms without the full advantages of the newer. The evidence compiled in 1904 indicated that railroad officers could expect an immediate reduction in direct operating costs of 30 to 40 per cent following the adoption of electrification, with the reduction growing steadily in magnitude as the system was expanded.[35]

The conservation of resources and environmental amenities was not a discovery of the 1960's, as the popular view holds. Gifford Pinchot's report outlining a federal conservation program was submitted to President Theodore Roosevelt in February, 1907, and the president acted on it with dispatch when he established

---

[35] W. B. Potter, for example, made a careful analysis of comparative operating costs for three representative freight-carrying lines and arrived at the following conclusions:

Total cost per engine mile (including depreciation)

Steam operation	$0.395
Electric operation	0.243
Reduction in cost	38.5 per cent

Total cost per 1,000 ton miles (including depreciation)

Steam operation	$0.707
Electric operation	0.496
Reduction in cost	29.9 per cent

Itemization of comparative costs per train mile for steam and electric operation

	Steam	Electric
Fuel for locomotive or power plant	$0.145	$0.103
Water	0.005	0.000
Wages of train crew	0.120	0.067
Maintenance	0.065	0.040
Supplies	0.005	0.002
Totals	0.340	0.212

Reduction in favor of electrical operation   37.6 per cent

(W. B. Potter, op. cit., p. 158.)

These reductions would have been greater if the companies that adopted electrification had made a more thorough use of centrally generated power for train heating and lighting, signaling, telegraph instruments, and telephones, as well as traction.

the Inland Waterways Commission in the following month. Railroad officers and their engineering lieutenants tended to think in narrowly financial terms, but there were some conspicuous exceptions (notably those having to do with the New York terminal programs) who thought in terms of a broad spectrum of public and urban benefits. It is doubtful whether anyone in the early years of the century inquired into the question of energy consumption per unit of transportation except to reduce costs and increase net income, but the calculations of an age more concerned with such matters may offer a guide. It was obvious to everyone that electric rail service provided immediate visible and tangible benefits to the comfort, health, and aesthetic environmental experience of passengers and urban dwellers, and while energy consumption was less obvious it had certainly begun to manifest itself to those responsible for such matters. The thermal efficiency of a steam locomotive seldom exceeded 6 per cent, a figure that does not to my knowledge take into account the transportation and handling of fuel or the impounding and pumping of water. The figures cited for the energy consumption of electric trains range from 1,300 B.T.U.'s per passenger mile for multiple-unit service to about 1,500 for operations with separate locomotives. The figure was undoubtedly much higher in 1905, possibly as high as 2,000 B.T.U.'s, but since the steam locomotive is a prime mover, calculations of comparable efficiency for electrification would have to comprehend the entire system, from coal entering the boiler at the power plant to the work performed by the locomotive.[36] The overall system efficiency was probably about 20 per cent for the largest installation of the time, but this figure would have risen in the case of the Long Island when the Hunter's Point plant was used to full capacity following the opening of Pennsylvania Station in 1910. Whatever the case, even the overall efficiency of an entire electrical installation was far superior to that of a steam locomotive.

On such questions as the technical uses and future possibilities of railroad electrification, the uses offering the best financial returns to the carriers, alternating current versus direct current, single-phase or polyphase systems, and the relative merits of overhead and third-rail distribution—these matters were considered at length by the authorities at congresses, conventions, and meetings of railroad and engineering societies, and their chief conclusions form part of the intellectual aspects

---

[36] As the inventory in note 32 indicates, such a calculation would have to take into account the respective efficiencies of boiler, turbine, generator, and switching in the power plant, converters and transformers in the substation, the transmission line, and the locomotive. Such figures as I have discovered are derived from Fowle, editor, Standard Handbook for Electrical Engineers. Others on energy consumption have been compiled by the United States Department of Transportation and the Bay Area Rapid Transit of San Francisco.

of this complex history. The technological issues would seem to have been most amenable to rational settlement, but they were far from that state in 1905. The two great controversies of the time had to do with the mode of distribution and the kind of current to be distributed.

The less pervasive of the two and the one for which experience offered a guide to relatively clear and unambiguous conclusions was the question of the third-rail distribution system as opposed to the overhead trolley. No standard main-line installation embodying the latter was to appear in the United States until the completion of the New Haven's program at New York in 1907, but proponents were vigorously urging its adoption during the planning stage of that very impressive achievement. Clement Street offered the most detailed presentation of both sides, and the weight of the evidence was against the third rail. Its shortcomings might be divided into technical practicalities, daily operations, and safety hazards. In the first category the obvious disadvantage was its interruption at switches and crossings of any description, and the associated need to shift the heavy iron or steel rail to the overhead position at concentrations of switches and crossovers in terminal areas, as was originally done at the Gare d'Orsay. Equally obvious was the inevitable interruption of service in severe snow and sleet storms. Installation and maintenance, even in places of accessibility, offered further difficulties: careful alignment, horizontality, and top surface free of irregularities were essential to prevent arcs but were diffcult to achieve and maintain. Parallel with this was the refractory problem of clearing locomotive running gear and cylinders and car trucks on one side of the rail and station platforms on the other. Track maintenance involving the renewal of rail and ties was not only rendered awkward and expensive but presented a constant danger even with the portable covers that the railroad adopted to protect track gangs. Beyond these were the clear safety hazards—displacement of the rail by a derailed locomotive or car, constant danger to employees and trespassers walking on the track, and the threat of fire in the event of a short-circuit following a derailment. There were technical objections to the overhead trolley, but they were less serious than those against the third rail. Inadequate headroom in tunnels and under bridges was solved by the retractable, spring-activated pantograph; breaks were more serious: not only could they oocur more easily, but breaks in the carrying wire or guy wires were likely to be as troublesome as those in the distributor itself. As for ice, the problem it presents has never been solved, and it simply must be regarded as an abnormal event requiring special *ad hoc* means to cope with it. The only telling argument against the trolley, actually, was the high initial cost, double the cost of installing third rail for a single track, with the cost rising more rapidly than the increase in number of

tracks. Once installed, however, it offered savings that balanced the expense in the long run.[37]

A more fundamental and more vehemently debated issue was the question of alternating current for locomotive motors as well as transmission, as opposed to the well intrenched direct-current distribution system. This involved the whole technology and economy of electric traction, and it remained a perfect stand-off until the New Haven again pointed the way in the 1907 program. The engineers had to resolve a broad complex of questions—the relative cost, size, weight, and efficiency of motors under the two kinds of current, problems of space limitations for motors and gearing or quills, the relative efficiency and cost of controls, the relative resistances of trolleys and third rails to electric current, the same for running rails when used as returns, the operation of alternating-current equipment on direct-current lines (as in the case of the New Haven at Grand Central Terminal), and finally, or perhaps overshadowing all else, the relative cost of distribution, transmission, and generating equipment.

W. B. Potter, an engineer in the railway department of the General Electric Company, provided the best summary of all the arguments at the time in a paper read before the New York Railroad Club on 20 January, 1905. At the time of this address, with the Long Island program still in process of installation, the system relying on high-voltage three-phase alternating-current transmission that was rectified and stepped down to direct current at low voltage by means of rotary converters and transformers in substations was the most widely used and the best known in the United States and Europe. On those roads on which alternating-current distribution and traction had been adopted or were being contemplated single-phase transmission and distribution were regarded as the best form in the United States, although three-phase applications were becoming common in Europe, particularly in Germany, Switzerland, and Italy. Experience in these countries indicated that the three-phase induction motor was well adapted to dynamic braking. On the foregoing basis Potter then proceeded into a detailed analysis of the relative merits of alternating and direct current.

The single-phase a. c. system possesses two features which recommend its use—economy of trolley copper, due to the higher trolley voltages, and the elimination of the rotary converter. . . . [The] saving in the initial cost . . . increases . . . in proportion to the amount of power required by each car or train and with the length of the trolley line. On the other hand, the a. c. equipments cost more than the d. c. . . . for a similar service and the same given rise in the temperature of the motors. It is therefore apparent that the relative cost of an a. c. or d. c. system will be materially affected by the number of cars employed.

The saving in power resulting in the elimination of the rotaries is about offset by the greater weight and the slightly lower efficiency of the a. c. motor.

[37] Clement F. Street, *op. cit.*. pp. 944–950.

The efficiency of the a. c. control during acceleration will . . . be somewhat higher than that of the d. c. system with series parallel control. With the a. c. system fractional voltages can be obtained from the transformer on the car. Each step of the a. c. controller therefore gives a running position which corresponds with the series and parallel positions in a d. c. controller. . . .

Resistance for 25-cycle alternating current, as compared to direct current, is about 50 per cent greater in the trolley wire and between six and seven times greater in the rail return. . . .

As the resistance of the track return with large steel rails is proportionately much less than that of the trolley wire, the apparent increase in resistance for the latter and the track taken together will be, roughly, from one-half to twice that for direct current. An alternating current of 1,000 volts is therefore about equivalent to 600 volts direct current so far as affecting the amount of trolley copper, and to secure the advantages of the a. c. system to a reasonable degree at least 3,000 volts, or, for heavier service, perhaps 5,000 volts must be employed.

The design of an a. c. motor as regards length of air gap and armature speed is affected by the lower average flux density.[38] For this reason an a. c. motor is larger and heavier than a d. c. unit of the same output. The commercial a. c. motor represents a compromise, in which the armature speed is somewhat higher and the air gap slightly less than would be the case in a d. c. motor of corresponding capacity. . . . The maintenance of an a. c. motor will . . . be greater than that of an equivalent d. c. motor, due both to the higher armature speed and the smaller air gap.

The equipment of heavy locomotives with a. c. motors for high-speed passenger service is a possibility, but owing to the limitations imposed by the space availability for the motors, it seems probable that two locomotives, each with four motors, would be required for service which could be performed by a single d. c. locomotive with four gearless motors. For locomotives in slow-speed work, such as freight or shifting, a double gear reduction will, in many cases, be required, owing to the difficulty of winding an a. c. motor of large size for slow speeds.

In view of the extensive application of the d. c. system, it is fortunate that the a. c. motor and its control may be so arranged as to be well adapted for operation on either high-potential alternating or 600 volt direct-current lines. . . . Equipments are not necessarily limited at all times to a particular route, and, further, where d. c. trolley lines are available, the expense of installing a special trolley is saved.[39]

Louis Duncan offered what by 1905 had become the traditional view of the relative merits of steam and electric traction in his presidential address to the convention of the American Institute of Electrical Engineers at Niagara Falls on 25 June, 1895, but his words were not widely known until they appeared in the *Railroad Gazette* ten years later. He was chiefly concerned with the considerable difference in the possibilities of electrification between passenger and freight operations, which of course was based on the limited experience of the time.

The [passenger] receipts of a road are increased by running trains at short intervals and at high speeds, and this is a condition peculiarly favorable to electricity. On an electric line short trains equally distributed over the track give a greater [generating] station efficiency, and the lowest cost of equipment of both station and lines. The cost of train service is somewhat greater, but is compensated by the saving in other items.

The cost of hauling a given number of passengers between given points by steam is greatly increased when the number of trains is increased, the efficiency is less, and the cost of equipment is greater.

On the other hand, . . . the conditions of the greatest economy [in freight operations] are reached when trains of a maximum weight are hauled by a single locomotive. The tendency in late years has been in the direction of increasing the size of the locomotive, the capacity of the cars and the length of the trains. The decreased cost per ton-mile . . . has shown the wisdom of the change. . . . In attempting to carry on traffic of this kind by electrical locomotives operating from a central station, we find that we are at a great disadvantage because of the irregular service necessitated by the freight traffic and the unequal distribution of load along the line. . . . The amount of freight transported per train-mile has more than doubled [1870–1890] and the expense has decreased more than one-half. The passengers per train-mile, on the other hand, have decreased and the expenses have changed only a slight amount. . . . Passenger traffic has come in the direction in which electricity is the most economical for transportation; freight traffic . . . has gone in the direction where electricity is the most costly. . . . The continuous current overhead trolley system is the only one that can be selected with a certainty of successful operation. It gives a minimum complication in the way of conveying the current to the cars, it allows a considerable range of speed with a comparatively high efficiency, and . . . successful operation could be at once guaranteed.[40]

But Duncan's view expressed the limited and cautious approach of the engineering and industrial mind in the early years, and his confidence in overhead distribution was not at the time borne out by the experience of the B. and O. and the New Haven (see Part I). Nine years later the electrical engineer and transportation planner Bion J. Arnold offered the clearest statement of the optimum operating conditions under which the electrification of steam railroads could be applied to the greatest advantage of the railroad company, presenting his views in his presidential address before the International Electrical Congress at Saint Louis on 14 September, 1904. He then went on to bold prophecies embodying permanently valid ideas.

The amount of energy transmitted to any great distance and used by electric cars on the roads that have been built up to the present time is small when compared with the amount of energy that it takes to propel a steam railroad train weighing 500 or 600 tons at the speeds ordinarily made by such trains. When investment is taken into consideration, power cannot be produced in a steam central

---

[38] The air gap is the space between the outer surface of the armature and the pole face of the field. Flux density is a measure of the intensity of the magnetic field over a given unit of area. It is affected by a property of the magnetic material known as magnetic permeability as well as current strength.

[39] W. B. Potter, *op. cit.,* pp. 156–157.

[40] Louis Duncan, *op. cit.,* pp. 444–446.

station, under conditions that exist today, and transmitted any great distance to a single electrically propelled train, requiring from 1,000 to 2,000 h. p., as cheaply as a steam locomotive . . . will produce the power necessary for its propulsion. . . . The ideal conditions for any trunk line railroad having a traffic heavy enough to warrant the investment in a sufficient number of tracks to properly handle this traffic in such a manner as to get the most efficient service out of its rolling stock, would be to have four or more tracks between terminal points arranged in pairs upon which the trains for different classes of service could be run at uniform rates of speed. Thus if six tracks were used, through . . . passenger and express service would be run on one pair of tracks; the local passenger, local express and local freight service upon another pair of tracks, while the through freight service would be run upon a third pair of tracks, and all the trains upon any pair of tracks would be run at the same average speed and stop practically at the same place.[41] If these conditions could prevail and the traffic were sufficient to warrant this investment in tracks, such a service could be operated more economically and more satisfactorily by electricity than by steam.[42]

In the same address Arnold then went on to sketch the future potentialities of rail electrification in details that carry full conviction today, especially in the United States, where politicians and corporation executives do not believe that the earth's energy resources are limited.

I am convinced that electricity will be generally used on our main railroad terminals, and ultimately on our main through lines for passenger and freight service, but it will not always be adopted on the grounds of economy of operation; neither will it come rapidly or through the voluntary acts of the owners of steam railroads, except in special instances. At first the terminals will be equipped . . . to effect economy in operation, or . . . through an increased demand on the part of the public for better service on the grounds that the use of the steam locomotive is objectionable in great cities. Those roads which run through populous countries will either build new roads, or acquire, for their own protection, those electric roads already built and operating in competition with them, and utilize them as feeders to their through line steam trains. . . . With these roads operating as feeders to the main line system and with the terminals thus equipped and the public educated to the advantages of riding in electrically equipped cars, the next step will logically be the electrical equipment of the trunk line between the cities already having electric terminals. . . . With . . . the desire on the part of the public for more prompt and effective freight service resembling that which is given by the steam roads in England and the Continent . . . there will be developed a high class freight service conducted in light, swiftly moving electric trains which can be quickly divided and distributed over the surface tracks of the smaller cities, or through underground systems similar to that which is now being built in Chicago.[43] . . . This class of freight service would soon prove so large a part of . . . freight traffic . . . that the operation of the through traffic by steam locomotives, though at present cheaper, would in time . . . grow less until [the] roads would ultimately use electricity exclusively. . . . With the single phase motor and steam turbines in successful operation and the transmission problem almost solved, and with the rapid development of the internal combustion engine now taking place, we are warranted in believing that we can combine them into a system which will ultimately supplant the steam locomotive in trunk line passenger and freight service.[44]

The philosophical issue, at least, was pretty well settled, even though the practical choices of the engineers continued to be far from unanimous. It remained for Clement Street, who was convinced of the unassailable and permanent superiority of electric traction, to give the last word in a paper presented to a meeting of the Western Railway Club at Chicago on 16 May, 1905. He found this superiority in seven essential features which can be summarized very simply: increased gross revenues through greatly improved service; a more efficient use of power; increased capacity of terminals; reduction in operating expenses (sufficient to yield a net income from suburban service); reduction in terminal costs; reduction in the maintenance costs of motive power; increased reliability.[45] He does not include the benefits to the human community of cleanliness, quietness, conservation of resources and land, and minimal interference with the urban fabric, but the public was already learning about such values and beginning to expect them.

---

[41] Only four railroad lines in the United States operated trains over continuous runs of some distance (as opposed to by-pass routes in large terminal areas) according to a segregated traffic pattern such as Arnold describes: Illinois Central, Chicago suburban terminal to Matteson, Illinois; Chicago and North Western, Chicago to Milwaukee (through passenger service abandoned); Pennsylvania, Trenton to Harrisburg via Philadelphia terminal zone; New York Central, Albany to Buffalo (former four-track line reduced to two). Of these only the Illinois Central line at Chicago fits the Arnold prescription exactly.

[42] Bion J. Arnold, *op. cit.,* pp. 414–415.

[43] The tunnel system underlying the Loop area in Chicago was constructed by the Illinois Telephone and Telegraph Company in 1901–1909. At one time it carried 70,000 cars of freight and rubbish per year, but in spite of the great and obvious value in relieving street congestion and atmospheric pollution, it was abandoned as a freight-handling facility.

[44] Bion J. Arnold, *op. cit.,* p. 415. The vision embraces the railroad segments of a balanced and hierarchical transportation system—street railways, interurban lines, trunk railroads—but most of it was sacrificed to jet and internal combustion engines.

For the place of the pioneer stage in the subsequent evolution of railroad electrification, see the following: "Evolution from Steam to Electric Traction," *Railway Age* **107**, 13 (23 September, 1939): pp. 440–443, 446, 449; "Fifty Years of Electric Traction," *loc. cit.* **118**, 23 (9 June, 1945): pp. 1018–1021; Reginald Gordon, "The Electrification of American Railways," *Engineering Magazine* **49**, 1 (April, 1915): pp. 34–42; William D. Middleton, *When the Steam Railroads Electrified* (Milwaukee, Kalmbach Publishing Company, 1974); F. H. Shepard, "Development of the Electric Locomotive," *Railway Age* **76**, 32 (14 June, 1924): pp. 1568–1569; *idem., Baldwin Locomotives* **10**, 1 (July, 1931): pp. 22–31; A. L. Stead, "Railway Electrification in the United States," *Railway Gazette* **43**, 7 (14 August, 1925): pp. 228–231 (concerned almost entirely with the New Haven programs over the previous thirty years). Of these works only the Middleton volume offers an adequate treatment of the subject.

[45] Clement Street, *op. cit.,* pp. 944–950.